Graham Rankin

MAGNOLIA

a hamlyn care manual

HAMLYN

Publishing Director
Laura Bamford
Creative Director
Keith Martin
Executive Editor
Julian Brown
Executive Art Editor
Mark Winwood
Editor
Karen O'Grady
Design
Ruth Hope
Production Controller
Clare Smedley
Picture Research
Wendy Gay
Special photography
David Loftus

First published in
Great Britain in 1999
by Hamlyn, a division of Octopus
Publishing Group Limited,
Michelin House, 81 Fulham Road,
London SW3 6RB

Copyright © 1999 Octopus
Publishing Group Limited

ISBN 0 600 59623 0

A catalogue record for
this book is available
from the British Library.

Produced by Toppan
Printed in China

Contents

Introduction

Introduction

We are so fortunate to have such a huge variety of plants at our disposal; unfortunately there is a tendency to take them for granted. During the middle of May when rhododendrons and azaleas put on their spectacular and dazzling display of colour, notable gardens bulge at the seams with an admiring public. The obsession and expectation for mass colour in gardens has blinded many to the subtle beauty of plants and the composition of their individual flowers.

Gardens should be planted to have some interest every month of the year. It is some of the early flowering plants that I consider to be the most precious, such as *Hamamelis mollis, Daphne bholua* and the numerous early-flowering rhododendrons, camellias and magnolias.

J.G. Millais (in his 1927 book on magnolias) said in praise of *Magnolia campbellii*, 'Its flowers are of such extraordinary beauty that once a plant has been seen at its best the beholder is enraptured that such a gem can be grown in our islands.'

Whilst a student, I visited The Royal Botanic Gardens, Kew in early March and saw for the first time a *Magnolia campbellii* in full flower. Never before had I seen a plant of such magnificence, and wondered why? The answer was simple, like the majority of people I was blissfully unaware of what delights gardens had to offer so early in the spring.

At that time I, like most people, perceived a magnolia as one of three plants, the widely planted *Magnolia x soulangeana*, the enchanting *Magnolia stellata*, or the stately evergreen *Magnolia grandiflora*. I had no idea of the diversity the genus had to offer, or how many different magnolias there were.

Magnolia flowers can be seen over nine months of the year, starting in early spring with the precocious Asiatic species and ending with *Magnolia grandiflora*, which will continue until the first frosts of autumn.

With skilful hybridisation, the size of the flower, the scent and range of colour has never been so diverse. Apart from the more usual whites and pinks, colours now include magenta, ruby-reds, metallic

Below: The author attending to a young *Magnolia campbellii* var. *alba*

blues and greens, tones of peach and apricot, through to the brightest of yellows.

The foliage is also spectacular, for example *Magnolia macrophylla* has the largest deciduous leaves of any woody plant that can be grown in temperate regions and the glossy- leaved evergreen species provide interest throughout the year. All these qualities, combined with the early age that some now attain florescence, have made magnolias more desirable than ever.

Every year several new cultivars are added to the 500 or more that are cur-rently available. With the exception of two plants, I have only written about some of the magnolias I have grown or seen, and have included those I consider worthy, with a few perhaps not so worthy, of cultivation.

I hope this book will arouse the interest and admiration of a group of plants that must rate as one of the most spectacular of all flowering trees and shrubs.

Left: A new yellow hybrid # 11/60 between *M. acuminata* x (*M. acuminata* x *M. denudata*) from the Brooklyn Botanic Garden Research Centre, as yet unnamed

Right: This specimen of *Magnolia campbellii* var. *mollicomata* at Lanhydrock in Cornwall is an unforget-table sight

History and Nomenclature

History

Evolutionary Beginnings

Fossil remains show that magnolias or members of the magnolia family grew in the Cretaceous period; this makes them the first flowering plants (Angiosperms) on earth. Before that time conifers and cycads (Gymnosperms) and, prior to those, the ferns and horsetails (Pteridophytes) dominated the landscape.

The spores of primitive non-flowering plants relied on wind for their dispersal. This is a very haphazard and wasteful way to distribute spores or pollen. Millions of grains of pollen can be produced from a single male conifer cone, for instance, most of which falls to the ground and is wasted.

The variety of insects was limited; the pollinators that we are familiar with now such as bees, butterflies and moths did not exist. Beetles, a primitive insect, were the early pollinators and now, 100 million years later, the pollination of magnolias is still carried out in the same way, almost exclusively by beetle-type insects. In order for the beetles to do this, they were attracted to the pollen in three ways: The sexual organs were surrounded with brightly coloured tepals. An appealing scent was emitted from the flower. The flowers provided edible sugary tissues and pollen as a food source.

One problem in having both male (androecium) and female (gynoecium) parts in one flower is the chance that the plant may pollinate itself, limiting genetic variation. To overcome this, the stigma (female) and the pollen (male) do not in fact reach maturity at the same time.

Above: In early summer the large bronze leaves of *Magnolia rostrata* give the appearance of a plant from a pre-historic era

Below: The cerise areas on the map show the present areas of natural distribution

The inner tepals of magnolia flowers can remain tightly closed for many days, providing a safe and sheltered environment for the beetles to feed. Whilst doing so they will place pollen on the receptive stigma. It is not until the stigmas are no longer receptive that the inner tepals open and the stamens release pollen which can be picked up by a passing beetle. This is an important consideration when breeding magnolias as it would be futile to try and pollinate an open flower.

Magnolias were once distributed over many parts of the world, but mainly in the northern hemisphere including Europe. During the last ice age when most plants in Europe perished, the flora of parts of Asia remained relatively unchanged. Today magnolias are confined within two geographic areas, eastern Asia and eastern America.

Magnoliaceae – The Magnolia Family

The family comprises of seven genera, and approximately 223 species, most of which are too tender for temperate climates. At one time it also included other closely related garden plants such as *Drimys, Illicium* and *Schisandra* but they have since been placed in other families. There are approximately 128 species of magnolias, a third of which can be grown in temperate climates.

The Name Magnolia

The name magnolia originates from the beginning of the eighteenth century. The genus was named to commemorate a French botanist, Pierre Magnol (1638-1715), who was Professor of Medicine and Prefect of the Botanical Gardens at Montpellier. The plant that was originally named to commemorate him was once called *Talauma*, a tropical plant from the West Indies in the same family. It was Linnaeus who unintentionally applied the name *Magnolia* to what we now know as *Magnolia virginiana*. Some authorities have recently renamed all the plants in the genus *Talauma* and now consider them as belonging to the genus *Magnolia*.

Above: Magnolias are often depicted in artwork, such as this *Magnolia grandiflora*

Opposite bottom: *Magnolia hypoleuca* has cone-like seedpods; this could well demonstrate the affinity between the magnolias and their evolutionary predecessors the conifers

Classification

The classification that is used today is based on the Binomial System of Nomenclature introduced by the Swedish botanist Carl von Linné (1707-1788) who wrote under the Latinised form of his name Carolus Linnaeus. This consists of a plant being given a double name consisting of two Latin words, the first being the name of the genus, the second the name of the species. Since this system was introduced, further categories have been added in order to distinguish any variance within the species.

The categories used in the naming of magnolias consist of:

Genus

A group containing related but distinct species e.g. *Magnolia, Michelia* and *Liriodendron*. These genera are linked together in the same family – Magnoliaceae.

Species

Plants of wild origin, which have characteristics common to each other, but distinct from others in the same genus, e.g. *Magnolia grandiflora, M. virginiana, M. wilsonii.*

Variety (var.)

This is used to define a botanical difference within a species which occurs naturally in the wild, e.g. var. *robusta,* var. *mollicomata,* var. *subcordata*

Cultivar

This is a compound word derived from CULTIvated VARiety and is used for plants that have been selected from plants in the wild, or from plants in cultivation, e.g. a hybrid, or a mutation which must be genetically stable. Cultivars should be written in roman not italic type and contained within single quotation marks, e.g. 'Exmouth', 'Susan', 'Yellow Bird'.

Magnolias sold with a cultivar name must not be raised from seed as they will not 'come true'.

The Plant's Name

If ever there was a confusing horticultural subject this is it. The reason is that the naming of plants is not a strict scientific study, but more of a subjective analysis, which is why plant names are constantly changing.

Plant names are governed by two sets of rules:

The International Code of Botanical Nomenclature (ICBN) which was last revised in 1994 these deal with the more scientific overview of the formation and use of plant names.

The International Code of Nomenclature for Cultivated Plants (ICNCP) first published in 1953 and last revised in 1995, this code is mainly concerned with the correct naming of 'man made' plants.

The purpose of these codes is to standardise internationally a correct procedure of naming and to clarify and put in order centuries of discordant names. The codes are very specific and are both amended every few years.

Magnolias have had their fair share of name changes since the first introductions.

Below: The beauty of the flower is enhanced by the arrangement of the reproductive organs, which are often overlooked

There are now over 100 invalid specific and variety names, for example; *Magnolia sprengeri, M. sprengeri* var. *elongata, M. sargentiana, M. biondii,* and *M. liliiflora* have all been described at some stage as the species *M. denudata.* The magnolia species *M. denudata* itself has had name changes, which in the past have included *Magnolia yulan, Yulania conspicua,* *Magnolia obovata, Magnolia obovata* var. *denudata, Magnolia precia, Gwillimia Yulan, Magnolia conspicua,* and *Magnolia heptapeta.*

Some names can also be misleading; one would assume that *Magnolia tripetala* had three petals (tepals); not so, it has between nine and sixteen.

Some authorities have now abandoned the species *M. stellata.* It has been the specific name for this plant since 1846 but at that time its generic name was

Buergeria. In 1872 it became *Magnolia stellata* and has remained unchanged since then. That is until 1954 when eminent botanists started to dispute its botanical status, and thought it should be classified as a variety of *M. kobus*. Observations were made of its seed-raised progeny, in which 50% of *M. stellata* seed produced plants typical of *M. kobus* with only a small fraction producing plants similar to its parent, the remainder being intermediate between the two. Another factor was the similarity in the floral characteristics and there is also doubt as to whether *M. stellata* is actually a species native to Japan, or possibly a plant of garden origin.

I cannot dispute the reasons for this possible reclassification, but it is a shame its original specific status could not be retained indefinitely, if for no other reason than its widespread use, familiarity and simplicity. In this book I have not adopted the possible change in its nomenclature and have continued to use the name *Magnolia stellata*, not *M. kobus* var. *stellata*, as it is now sometimes called.

One further problem is that if *M. stellata* was considered a variety of *M. kobus*, it also affects the name of the hybrids known as *M. x loebneri* which have *M. kobus* as one parent and *M. stellata* (or any of their respective cultivars) as its other parent. Some authorities consider that these hybrids should also be given variety status so is referred to as *M. kobus* var. *loebneri*. Again, in this book I shall retain its more commonly known name. No doubt it will be several years before this taxonomic and nomenclatural dilemma is sorted out.

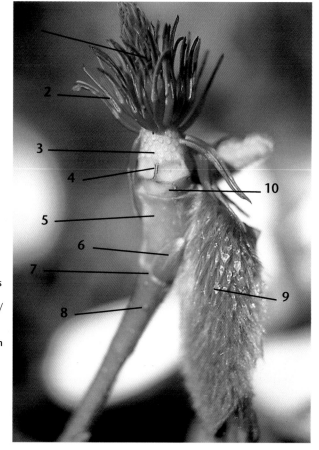

Right: The main floral parts of a magnolia without tepals

1. Gynoecium/stigmas
2. Stamens
3. Androecium
4. Tepal scars
5. Pedicle
6. Leaf bud
7. Node
8. Lenticels
9. Perule
10. Annular scar

Petals and Tepals

It is not only magnolia names that can be changed. In 1950 it was decided that magnolias no longer had petals. Most plants have a calyx, which is situated at the base of the flower and once enclosed the flower bud, and each segment of the calyx is called a sepal. Some plants, such as tulips and crocus, do not have a calyx at all. Whilst sepals are absent on some species of magnolia, on others such as *Magnolia liliiflora* they are quite prominent and measure up to 3.5cm (1¼in) in length.

Mr. J.E.Dandy, an eminent botanist of the Natural History Museum London, who was considered the world botanical authority of the genus, decided that because the sepals and the petals of magnolias were not easily differentiated, they should collectively be called tepals. The term tepal has been universally adopted and has been used in every publication on magnolias since.

HISTORY AND NOMENCLATURE

15

The Plant Hunters

MAGNOLIA *altissima Lauro cerasa folio flore ingenti candido* The Laurel leaved Tulip tree.

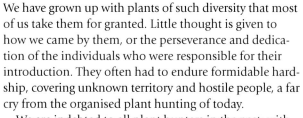

Most of the American species have now been cultivated in Britain for two centuries.

Early records are unclear as to which magnolia was the first from Asia. Both *Magnolia denudata* and *Magnolia coco* were introduced approximately a century later.

It was Sir Joseph Banks, a botanist and amateur scientist of wealth who sailed with Captain Cook on his first voyage around the world, who introduced *Magnolia denudata* in 1780. All known temperate Asian magnolias are now in cultivation, the most recent introductions being *Magnolia zenii, Magnolia biondii* and *Magnolia amoena.*

During the twentieth century, two men in particular have made a great contribution, introducing many of the magnificent Asiatic magnolia species which adorn our gardens today.

George Forrest

George Forrest (pictured on previous page) was born at Falkirk, Scotland in 1873. It was while he was working in the herbarium at the Royal Botanic Gardens at Edinburgh, that the opportunity came to travel abroad in the quest of plants. He was sponsored by eminent wealthy horticulturists of the time, who were the recipients of what was collected.

George Forrest, in *The Gardeners Chronicle* of 1910, wrote an account

We have grown up with plants of such diversity that most of us take them for granted. Little thought is given to how we came by them, or the perseverance and dedication of the individuals who were responsible for their introduction. They often had to endure formidable hardship, covering unknown territory and hostile people, a far cry from the organised plant hunting of today.

We are indebted to all plant hunters in the past; without them our gardens would certainly be devoid of the colour, scent, interest and beauty to which we are now so accustomed.

The earliest introductions of magnolia came to Britain from America. John Bannister, a missionary who was sent to Virginia, introduced *Magnolia virginiana* in 1688.

of plant hunting in China entitled: *'The Perils of Plant Collecting'*.

He said, 'Living in China is like camping alongside an active volcano', and during 1905 whilst collecting in the N.W. corner of the Chinese province of Yunnan, the 'volcano' erupted. The Lama region was unsettled by the invasions of the British and Chinese, and any foreigner was considered a threat and therefore unwelcome.

The situation was getting far too serious and he knew he had to get out quickly. He travelled mainly at night trying to elude the watchfulness of the hostile armed Tibetans, but 'was hunted like a wild beast'. On the second day of the chase he discarded his boots to avoid leaving distinctive trails and slept where he could, one night under a log in the bed of a stream.

Of his team of 17 collectors and helpers only one escaped.

He became totally exhausted and states: 'At the end of eight days I had ceased to care whether I lived or died - my feet swollen out of all shape, my hands and face torn with thorns, and my whole person caked with mire. I was nearly dead through hunger and fatigue and on the evening of the eighth day and

Above: The beautiful *Magnolia* 'Forest Pink' was introduced by George Forrest, but its origins are unclear. The seed may have been collected from a cultivated plant

Right: *Magnolia campbellii* var. *alba* and *Rhododendron kesangiae* growing in their native habitat in Bhutan

morning of the ninth was quite delirious for a time. Then I knew the time was near, and determined to make one more bid for life.

In the valley there happened to be two small villages of four to six huts each, peopled by Lissoos, a sub-tribe of Tibetans, and I decided to hold up one of these, to force the inhabitants to give me food. This plan I carried out on the evening of the ninth day. Fortunately instead of opposing me, the people proved friendly.

The one and only food of these people consists of parched barley or wheat coarsely ground; it is called 'tsaniba'. This they offered me, and having but little self-control, after such a long stave, I partook of it ravenously, in fact to such an extent that I almost died of the effects. As it was, to add to my trials, I brought on inflammation of the stomach, from which I suffered for many months.'

The headman of the village made arrangements to smuggle him out of the country with the aid of native hunters. This took several days through

Ernest Henry Wilson ('Chinese Wilson')

Born in 1876 in Chipping Campden, Gloucestershire, at the age of 13 he left school to become an apprentice gardener. At 16 he went to work at Birmingham Botanical Gardens, and after four years went on to The Royal Botanic Gardens, Kew. When he was 22 he left Kew to study botany at the Royal College of Science in South Kensington. A year later he was in China working for the famous nursery, James Veitch & Sons at Chelsea.

From 1906 until his death, he worked for the Arnold Arboretum, Boston, USA.

By the age of 46 he had spent eight years in China, but he also travelled extensively to other countries including America, Japan, Korea, Taiwan, India, Australia, New Zealand and South Africa.

Wilson introduced over 1,000 plant species into cultivation; we probably grow in our gardens more of his introductions than any other collector. These include well-known plants such as *Actinidia deliciosa* (kiwi fruit), *Cornus kousa* var. *chinensis, Davidia involucrata* (handkerchief tree), *Lilium regale* and sixty species of rhododendron. The magnolia species he introduced were *M. wilsonii, M. dawsoniana, M. delavayi, M. sprengeri, M. officinalis,M. sinensis, M. sargentiana* and its variety *M. s. robusta* - a greater number than any other plant hunter.

Tragically, in 1930, Ernest Wilson and his wife died when their car spun off the road.

downpours of rain, almost no food or shelter, walking over glaciers, snow and jagged limestone strata, which tore his feet to ribbons. When he had almost reached safety, he trod on a bamboo spike, which penetrated through his foot and he suffered excruciating agony for many days.

It was on his seventh expedition to China in 1932, whilst out shooting, that he collapsed and died.

Apart from the butterflies, birds and anthropological material, he managed to collect over 31,000 plants, which included eight species of magnolia, three of which were new to cultivation. The collections came from Yunnan, Myanmar (Burma) and Tibet, and included the species *Magnolia campbellii* var. *mollicomata* and its cultivar 'Lanarth', *M. nitida, M. rostrata, M. globosa,*

Above: *Magnolia wilsonii* **was discovered by Ernest Wilson in 1904 in western Szechwan. A charming species with pendulous flowers that open during late spring and early summer**

Opposite: Along with many rhododendron species, Sir Joseph Hooker also introduced *Magnolia campbelli* **in 1849**

Propagation

Although the range of magnolias available from specialist nurseries has never been greater, considering how many different and superior forms there are the choice is still very limited. Anyone serious about growing a large number should consider propagating their own plants. Admittedly, it can be frustrating at times but the sense of achievement far outweighs the occasional disappointment.

No one expects a 100 per cent success rate, so it is sensible to propagate more than you need. Inevitably you will end up with a surplus of plants, and it is then you can share one of the great joys of gardening, the giving and receiving of plants from fellow enthusiasts.

Seed Sowing

Most magnolia species produce seed in Britain. Seedpods are ready to collect during the early autumn. In British gardens the quantity of seed produced varies tremendously from year to year, depending on various environmental conditions.

It is best to collect the pods just before they open up to reveal the bright orange/red seeds inside. If the seeds fall to the ground rodents and other seed-eating animals

quickly consume them. A single pod, which can measure up to 20cm (8in), may contain over 100 seeds.

The germination of magnolia seed is very easy, as long as the following guidelines are used.

After removing all the seeds from the pod, which may be assisted by the use of a blunt instrument such as a screwdriver, it is imperative that the orange-red outer coating is removed. This is best achieved by placing the seeds in water for two or three days. After that time, when the seed coat is squeezed the hard black seed will be forced out, sometimes at great speed! It is this fleshy, oily, orange-red coating that prevents the absorption of water to the embryo and inhibits the seed from germinating. The reverse is also true in that it prevents the seed from losing moisture, so that as soon as the

Right:
Cleaned seeds are usually black or dark brown. Pictured are seeds of *Magnolia delavayi* which have started to germinate. The radicle (root) has just started to appear

Opposite:
Successful germination of magnolia seed

Below:
Collect the seedpods before the red seeds are visible. This will ensure that no seeds are lost

layer has been removed it is essential that the seeds are kept damp, or they will perish very quickly. This is usually the case when magnolia seed is purchased from commercial seed suppliers, as it invariably does not germinate.

After the fleshy coat is removed, wash the seeds in some dishwashing liquid to remove the oily film that is left. Put the seeds in a bag containing a damp, sterile medium such as peat or, preferably, Cornish grit, seal and label and put in a domestic refrigerator with an ideal temperature between 1-5°C (34-41°F).

Sow the seed in late February under glass, at a temperature of 18-20°C (64-68°F). For large quantities a seed tray is ideal, approximately 100 seeds can be germinated in a 36 x 22cm (14 x 8½in) tray which should have a minimum depth of 7cm (3in). A flowerpot can

be used for smaller quantities. They can also be sown singly in a cellular tray, theoretically minimising root disturbance but, apart from taking up a lot of space, the compost within each cell is prone to drying out as watering is more difficult. They do not resent the root disturbance when pricked-out in the conventional manner.

The compost is the same as that used for cuttings, a 50/50 mix of Irish moss peat and Cornish grit; this is more open than one would usually use for seed sowing, but is ideal for magnolias. As the seedlings have a thick, brittle root system, when you prick-out the sowing medium falls away from the roots, which makes the roots easy to untangle from each other and fewer losses occur. The compost

also contains very little nutrient, but as seedlings are ready for pricking-out only four weeks after germinating, this is not necessary.

Sow the seed evenly, cover the seed with 1cm (½in) of compost and water in. Cover the tray or pot to maintain the moisture and to protect the seed.

The seed germinates from four weeks, but can take up to four months. They are ready for pricking out after the first true leaves develop, which is usually four to eight weeks after germination. During this time the young seedlings need to be shaded on bright, sunny days. If the germination rate is very low, prick out what comes up and leave the seeds that have not germinated in the tray undisturbed. Keep them watered throughout the summer and protect from mice. It is possible that the seed left may germinate the following spring.

Do the pricking out on an overcast day and water immediately after potting up. If warm, sunny weather is forecast soon afterwards, cover the plants with a thin plastic sheet to keep them humid and shade from direct sunlight. It is important to reduce the amount of transpiration at this vulnerable stage. Spraying the foliage occasionally with water will also help. As with all pricking-out, handle the seedlings by the leaves, never by the stem.

Pot the seedlings into small pots, with a proprietary ericaceous compost and feed throughout the growing season with either a slow-release fertilizer, or with a foliar feed specifically for acid-loving plants.

Cuttings

Because of technological advances in propagating techniques, this is the most-used method for producing magnolias commercially. The use of computerised propagation facilities has made rooting of the more difficult plants easier. These computerised systems control the heating, shading and humidity. Most propagators use mist or fog systems to maintain an accurate level of humidity, which is invaluable for plants that take a long time to root. Because of the high humidity, transpiration is reduced to a minimum and the cuttings do not become stressed.

The propagation of magnolias from cuttings has several advantages:
• Because this is a form of vegetative propagation, the resulting plant is identical to the parent.
• Vegetatively propagated plants flower at a younger age than seed-raised plants.
• It is much easier and requires less skill and than grafting.
• Plants raised on their

own roots can sometimes grow better.
• No suckers are formed.

Some magnolias root very easily from cuttings, and it is not necessary to have expensive facilities to achieve a good success rate. With easy species such as *M. liliiflora* and *M. stellata*, all that is needed is a pot with a plastic bag tied over the top, placed in a warm room away from direct sunlight. If a misting system is not used a 'closed case' environment can still be very satisfactory.

For most amateurs a small propagator is very useful; these are very simple to construct or can be purchased ready-made at most garden centres. The most important feature is a soil warming cable with a thermostat; this can keep the temperature around the base of the cutting at an ideal temperature of

1. The leaves of the cuttings should be cut cleanly in half on a wooden board. This reduces transpiration during the rooting process

between 21-23°C (70-73°F). All cuttings root more quickly if they have bottom heat.

As the air temperature increases the relative humidity drops. Cuttings can tolerate high temperatures with a high humidity, but high temperatures and low humidity cause instant disaster. The cuttings need a very high humidity because they do not yet have roots for the uptake of water, but as they have leaves transpiration still takes place. If humidity is low the plants lose more water than they can absorb which causes them to wilt and die. Keeping the cuttings in an enclosed environment retains moisture and produces ideal conditions.

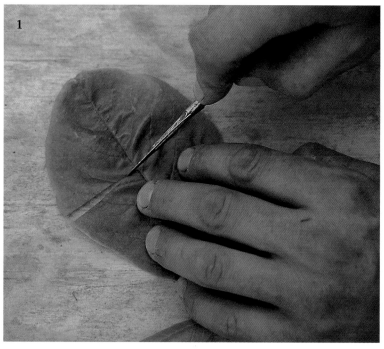

2. The soft terminal growth is removed just above a bud. If this is not done it will inevitably perish and increase the chance of fungal infection

3. The cut at the base of the cutting must be made just below a bud. The bud is then cut away to 'wound' the plant

4. The finished cutting ready for insertion into a hormone powder or dip

The Cutting

Cuttings are best taken from early to mid summer. Any earlier than that the wood will be too soft and will be susceptible to infection; later on the wood becomes more difficult to root, and the plant may not get established enough to survive the dormant season. The mother plant must be healthy and not under any water stress. Cuttings also root better if the mother plant is young and vigorous.

If you can, choose a day that is cool and overcast, place the cuttings in a plastic bag, and do not delay in preparing them. Cuttings can be transported successfully for a few days by putting them in a dampened sandwich bag and stored in a cooled picnic bag, but do not allow the cuttings to come into direct contact with the ice blocks.

When taking the cutting use the current season's growth, without any flowers or flower buds on it. It is good practice to make the cut just above a node , as the section of wood left on the mother plant will die back to that point anyway.

Cut the piece of wood at least two nodes longer than you require the cutting to be. The length you take depends on the type of plant. Somewhere between 8-12cm (3¼-5in) allows you to reduce it in size when you prepare it ready for the propagator. As magnolias do not root as easily from internodal cuttings, use the ends of the growths.

Preparing the Cutting

The best tool for this is the same one as for grafting, the scalpel. The use of such a sharp blade can be rather off-putting. If you are not conversant with the technique of using sharp knifes for cuttings, ask a competent professional to demonstrate the technique. Alternatively, place the cuttings on a piece of wood and draw the blade across the wood. Do not simply push down and guillotine the cutting, as this will cause bruising and subsequent rotting of the soft tissue.

Firstly, cut all the leaves off apart from the top three or four. Remove the soft terminal growth, including the undeveloped young leaf, down to the dormant bud just above the next leaf petiole. If this is not done this soft growth is likely to rot.

The Rooting Medium

This is the same as for seed sowing: a 50/50 mixture of Irish moss peat and Cornish grit. To date I have not had such a good success rate with the peat alternatives I have tried. The use of Cornish grit by itself also gives good results, particularly when a mist or fog system is used. However, as this is a very open mix, firm the medium in the propagating tray very well before the cuttings are inserted. The use of a dibber is also advisable on the thinner, softer cuttings to avoid damage when inserting.

Aftercare

Unless the cutting is from a plant of the smallest leafed varieties, the remaining two or three leaves should be cut in half, which reduces transpiration during the rooting process. The basal cut must be made just below a node at an angle of 45 degrees. The base of the cutting must also be 'wounded'; this is done by removing a thin strip of wood including the bud near the base on one side, and just a strip of bark on the other. There are three advantages in doing this: it exposes more cambium, from which the roots start to grow; it allows an increase of water uptake whilst in the rooting medium; it increases the absorption of the rooting hormone if used.

The base of the cutting can then be placed in a hormone powder of a suitable strength, which contains a fungicide.

Hormone powders do not have a long shelf life so ensure the one you use is not old. Liquid hormone treatments or 'dips' are also available which work very well.

If several different varieties are being inserted into the same tray, put the easier rooting types together so there is less disturbance to the more difficult ones which are staying in the tray. Firm around the base of each cutting after insertion and water in the cuttings as soon as you have finished. The addition of a suitable fungicide to the water at this stage is also beneficial. If for some reason there is any delay in preparing the cuttings, or during periods of high temperatures, spray water on them at regular intervals with a hand-held sprayer to ensure they remain fresh.

Above: A tray of rooted *Magnolia grandiflora* cuttings ready for potting

Rooting is very slow, so nothing will happen for the first month apart from callusing around the cambium of the wound. On a daily basis check the moisture level of the rooting medium and remove leaves that have dropped off the cuttings. Also check to see if any of the cuttings are turning black or brown at compost level, this often happens if the rooting medium is kept too wet, or the growth was too soft. Remove the rotting cuttings as soon as possible as the fungal infection may spread. Usually the first sign is that the leaves go yellow and drop off.

During the second month small roots should start to form from the callusing. After eight weeks some may be ready to be put into small pots, although others may have just started to show signs of rooting. It is now that the importance of keeping similar types together is apparent. If it is not possible to use a separate propagating tray for each type, leave a large gap between types so the cuttings that are left do not have their fragile developing roots disturbed. If rooted cuttings are removed from a tray leaving some cuttings with undeveloped root systems, fill the tray up again with rooting medium so that remaining cuttings have adequate medium to root into and also to maintain constant moisture and temperature levels within the tray. Even under perfect conditions one seldom achieves 100 per cent rooting.

There is less chance of losses during the winter if the rooted cuttings are left undisturbed in the trays, and potted up in the spring. It is important that all trays and pots must be protected from frost, as leaving them in an unheated greenhouse during very cold spells can freeze the roots and kill them.

Very often plants are neglected in a greenhouse during these months, and many plants die as a result. It is surprising how quickly the compost or rooting medium can dry out during the winter so check periodically to make sure the compost is always slightly damp. Over-watering plants can also cause the plant to die.

If the easily rooted types are potted on immediately after rooting, they must be placed back into a humid environment for a few days and ideally removed on an overcast day so they can slowly acclimatize to normal conditions. Harden off the plants quickly, because if the growth is too lush and soft at the onset of winter, it will be susceptible to infection and die-back.

Grafting

The art of grafting was known to be practised by the Chinese as early as 1,000 BC, although it was not until the sixteenth century that grafting was widespread in England. During the nineteenth century over one hundred methods were known and described. Every propagator has a different technique and each advocates a multitude of alternative practices.

Grafting is best performed by someone with dexterity and a cool temper. This form of propagation requires more skill than taking cuttings or sowing seed, but is by far the most rewarding when you become proficient.

All grafting must be carried out with a clean, razor-sharp knife, since no matter how skilful the grafter's hand, a blunt knife gives a low percentage of takes. I find a Swann-Morton scalpel with a number 26 surgical blade the ideal instrument (these are available from most art and craft shops). When using a knife keep arms tight into the body for stabilitly

As long as some basic principles are followed, the chance of success is good. It has to be said that even experts would not consider magnolias the easiest of plants. Results can be inconsistent; what can appear to be the 'perfect' graft may not take. This is probably due to the very soft, pithy wood which is easy to bruise, so being susceptible to infection. Even after the union is callused over, some scions seem reluctant to grow.

Late winter is the best time to graft. The two methods I use have been adopted over many years and seem to be well suited for magnolias.

The reasons for grafting plants are:
• Some magnolias are very difficult or seemingly impossible to root from cuttings.
• Because this is a vegetative form of propagation the plant will be true to type.
• In the short term it will usually produce a larger plant in less time than cuttings.
• If you need to exchange or send plant material, it is much easier to send scions as they travel better than cuttings.
• You can use every bud and terminal growth on the scion to make a new plant, assuming you have the correct size of stock to match.
• Grafting can be carried out at the end of the dormant season, utilising a slack time of year.

Definition of Terms

The Scion
This is the piece of wood that has been taken from the plant you wish to propagate. It has several dormant buds and it is these that, when united with the stock, form the stem and eventually, the branches of the new plant.

The scion must be taken from the growth that was made during the previous season. Select a vigorous, straight growth, without a flower bud at the end. Avoid taking material that comes from the very base of the plant just in case it is rootstock that has grown unnoticed. It is best to use the buds from the top 30cm (1ft) of the scion, the growth below that will be too thick and woody. Keep the scions cool and damp and, if collecting more than one type, ensure they are labelled as soon as they are cut.

The Stock (rootstock or understock)
This is the lower part of the union that will be the root system of the new plant. It is usually a plant raised from seed.

The preparation needs to start at least a year in advance with the growing of the rootstock. It is important that the rootstock used should be of the same eventual growth habit. In the past some commercial growers have

Below: Irrespective of what plant you take cuttings from, always remove the flower buds and certainly never let them flower such as these

used rootstocks which have been of a slower rate of growth than the scion. This has a tendency to induce flowering at an earlier age, and can have a dwarfing effect on the plant. Although the graft makes a satisfactory union, after a few years it becomes noticeable that the scion increases its girth faster than the rootstock, this causes a weak union and eventually it is likely to snap.

One of the most important factors in successful grafting is the condition of the rootstock. It must be of vigorous growth and free from pests, particularly red spider mite, which could have laid its orange eggs on the stem at the end of the previous season (see Pests and Diseases, page 66). The stocks must not be more than two years old, and for ease of handling a pot size of one litre is ideal.

The rootstocks are brought into a warm greenhouse at least two weeks before the grafting is to take place, this induces the buds to swell but must not be so advanced as to bring the plant into leaf. It is wise to check the condition of the roots of each stock before grafting. All the roots should be cream-coloured; if they are brown discard the plant.

Now comes the tricky bit, for when grafting takes place the compost in the pot must be only slightly moist so as to minimise the flow of sap. If it is too wet, the wound will bleed and this will cause the graft to fail. Just a bit too dry and the roots will dry out followed by the death of the rootstock.

The Graft

Chip Budding
The benefit of using this technique is twofold:
1 Every bud on the scion can be used, so as many as ten grafts can be made from a scion that is 30cm (1ft) long.
2 The knife-work and the carpentry involved are much easier.

It involves cutting a bud no longer than 3cm (1¼in) long from the scion. The first cut is made 1cm (½in) below the bud; this cut can be deeper than necessary. The second cut which starts no more than 2cm (¾in) above the bud must be as straight as possible. Try to draw the blade down and across the scion using the full length of the blade, this will produce a cleaner cut. As the second cut meets the first the chip may fall, so place a sheet of paper on the bench so that the chip remains clean.

The next step is to cut another chip of the same size out of the stock, as near to the base as practicable. If you

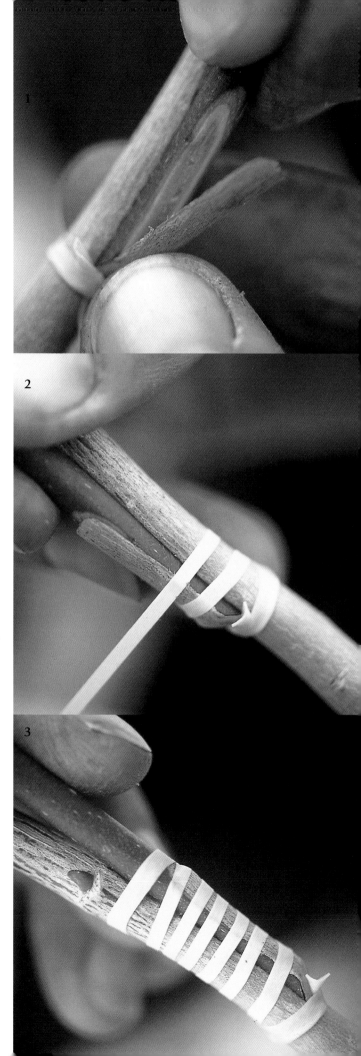

1. The incision on the stock plant to create a flap of wood that will cover the scion. Tie the grafting band just below the base of the wound ready for tying in the scion

2. Practice tying the grafting band before you start grafting, it is not as easy as it looks. Being under tension it is easy to let go when finishing tying off

3. The completed side graft with the stock and scion matching perfectly

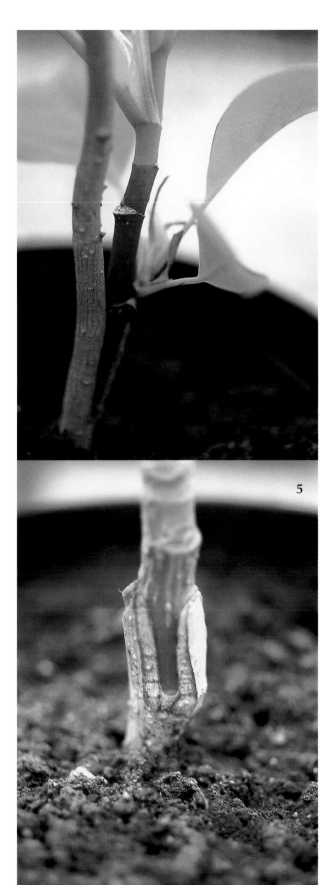

4. A two month old side graft. Note the use of the bend in the stock plant to achieve a better union

5. A year old side graft showing good cambium growth around the union. The top of the stock plant on the left hand side has been cut away so no snags are left

are unpractised at this it is useful to hold the piece of scion from where the first chip was removed against the stock where the second chip is to be taken, which gives you an accurate guide for size. At this stage, tie a strip of grafting tape, or a cut rubber band, just below where the chip on the stock was taken. Pick up the chip from the scion without touching the cut surface using the protruding bud if it is large enough; if not, the scalpel blade can be used as a spatula to help place the chip onto the matching surface on the stock. Tie together, wrapping the band around the stem and the chip, to hold them secure.

Side Grafting

The carpentry involved in this grafting is not easy and practice is needed before attempting it. This technique uses the last 6cm (2½in) of the terminal growth on the scion. Choose a stock that is of a slightly larger size than the scion. It is often useful to take advantage of any slight outward curve near the base of the stock which will allow the stock and the scion to make a better fit.

The base of the scion is cut at an angle of 45 degrees with a cut made on either side, a longer cut being made on the side against which it will be matched to the stock. A corresponding cut is made on the rootstock near the base (opposite a slight outward curve if it has one), leaving a flap.

One end of the grafting band is tied below the cut of the stock. Place the scion in the cut; cover the scion with the flap. The band is then wrapped around the graft and tied, securing the scion in place, checking that the wounds match on both sides.

Aftercare

The aftercare is the same for both the chip and budding and side grafting methods. To achieve rapid callusing (the growth of cambium cells joining the stock and scion) the grafted plants should then be put into an environment which is very humid and kept at a constant temperature of between 24-26°C (75-79°F). This is achieved by putting them in a 'closed case'. These are sold as propagating cabinets and can be purchased from garden centres, but ensure they incorporate a thermostat for temperature control and a high cover of at least 40cm (1½ft). They can also be made easily and cheaply using a soil warming cable, a timber frame and plastic to cover the structure.

Cover the soil warming cables with enough peat for the pots to be 'bedded' in. It is important to keep the peat damp at all times, firstly to ensure that the roots do not dry out completely, secondly to keep a very high humidity, and thirdly to prevent the soil warming cables from burning out, as peat is very insulating when dry.

It is often recommended that the graft union is covered in wax to avoid moisture entering the union and causing infection. I have found that it is easier to lay strong absorbent kitchen towelling over the grafted plants, so that any condensation which drips from the cover does not fall onto the graft union. The towelling should be used until the union is callused.

While the callusing takes place no watering should be necessary. After two weeks check the plants are not too dry; if they are, just a slight dampening is necessary. After three weeks, callusing (the growth of tissue around the cut surfaces) will be very noticeable. It is only now that you can start the normal watering regime and increase ventilation. As soon as the bud starts to grow the graft tie should be carefully removed. At this stage the rootstock is cut back to 15cm (6in) above the graft to encourage the shoot to put on growth. After this initial cutting back of the rootstock, it must not be cut again until early summer, because you would get severe bleeding from the wound.

If any of the chip buds or scions turn black remove it at once to avoid the spread of any fungal infections. After a week of increasing ventilation, the plants can be moved to a shaded part of the greenhouse. The temperature of the greenhouse should be kept warm to encourage growth. They can now be potted into a larger pot.

As the new shoot grows, gently tie it in to the piece of rootstock that is left to keep the new growth straight, at the same time removing all the new shoots that come from the rootstock.

When the new shoot has put on 15-20cm (6-8in) of growth, which should be by early to mid-summer, the remaining rootstock can be cut away to just above the graft union. The new growth must then be tied to a thin stake to ensure the plant continues to grow straight.

Summer Grafting Using the Chip Budding Method

This is best carried out in mid to late summer, using the dormant buds above the leaf petiole (stalk). The stock should be cut back to 30cm (1ft) for ease of handling and to reduce transpiration while the compost dries out. As the flow of sap has slowed down during this time of year, the wound does not bleed as much, so the compost does not need to be quite as dry as in late winter grafting.

1. The first cut is made below the leaf scar and can be made deeper than needed. The second cut is being made as straight as possible behind the bud

2. It is helpful to hold the section of wood where the bud was removed alongside the stock plant to give an accurate guide to the size of wood to remove from the stock

3. Tie the grafting band on the stock before placing the chip in the stock. It is necessary to gently ease open the base of the wound on the stock with the blade of the scalpel while inserting the chip to ensure a snug fit

4. The finished graft which must not have any gaps or spaces around the edge

5. Remove the grafting band carefully after the wound has callused and the bud has started to swell, this should be within four weeks of grafting

As the scion wood is in full leaf, the leaves are cut off immediately upon collection, leaving just 1cm (½in) of the leaf petiole. This provides a useful handle to hold the chip and also acts as an early indicator for a successful union. This 'handle' should not perish but fall off cleanly after the union has callused.

Unlike late winter grafting the scion does not grow away vigorously, but may only grow a few centimetres during that season.

Layering

Although this is the oldest method of vegetative propagation, it is very seldom practised nowadays. It involves rooting the end part of a branch in the ground while it is still attached to the mother plant. Magnolias can layer themselves without any intervention, particularly when they have not been pruned correctly and branches have been allowed to rest on the ground.

Layering is best carried out before growth commences in the spring. Prepare a small area of the ground by mixing in some peat and grit. Select the end part of the branch that is near to the ground and 'wound' it where the start of last year's growth meets the previous year's growth. Push a stout cane into the prepared area so the leader can be tied to it. Place the wounded piece of stem 6cm (2¼in) below the surface, peg down and tie in the leader. It usually takes two to three years before the plant can be cut away from the mother plant and dug up for use elsewhere.

Micropropagation or Tissue Culture

This method is used extensively and with great success to propagate a wide range of plants, but unfortunately magnolias in general have not proved to be very responsive to this form of propagation. However, there have been successes and these have been commercially produced for the past decade. At present they only represent a small fraction of plants sold, but given time this figure will no doubt increase.

The technique is carried out in a laboratory under sterile conditions. A minute tip of a vigorous growing shoot (although most parts of a plant can be used) is placed on a sterile growing medium containing nutrients and growth hormones; this produces a callus tissue, which can be continuously subdivided. These cells are then placed on to another growing medium, which stimulates them into producing shoots and eventually roots are formed.

Buying

The phrase, 'Buyer Beware' must have originated amongst disillusioned magnolia growers, not the second-hand car market as I had always thought!

The majority of magnolias are bought on impulse during the spring when they are in flower. The advantage of this is that you can see what the plant is like and compare them to others. However, the more sought-after plants are very quickly snapped up, so ordering in advance is advisable.

Unlike many trees such as oaks, eucalyptus and conifers, magnolias do not develop a taproot. Buying small plants is not a disadvantage, in fact on the contrary, not only are they cheaper, they often establish themselves more quickly when planted.

Magnolias can be purchased from most garden centres, but the range is usually limited and unfortunately they always tend to sell the same varieties. Their selection is based on what the wholesalers can supply, which in turn depends on ease of propagation for the grower. This is understandable, but the tendency is to keep to the tried and tested plants that have been propagated since time immemorial. They are not usually the better cultivars.

Previous page: *Magnolia sprengeri* var. 'Diva' at Cambridge University Botanical Gardens

Below: Specialist nurseries and plant centres are by far the best places to buy a wide range of plants. They usually sell the newer and better cultivars

Unfortunately, in the case of magnolias, it can literally take decades for new cultivars to be available through garden centre outlets.

To acquire the better forms, it is necessary to go to more specialist nurseries, of which there is an increasing number. The RHS Plant Finder, which is updated every year, is an invaluable reference book to source specific plants. It is available at most bookshops or public libraries. Altogether it lists over 70,000 plants, which includes all the magnolias available in Britain and the nurseries that sell them.

A most important consideration when buying a plant is to check that it is correctly labelled. Unfortunately, all too often plants are purchased which are not what the labels state they are.

Some nurseries have had a deplorable reputation for selling magnolias in the past. The worst crime is to sell seedlings of named cultivars under the pretence that they are the "real thing". It would be nice to think that it was a crime of the past, but alas it still goes on, even at garden centres of high reputation. All magnolias with a cultivar name must be propagated vegetatively by cuttings, grafting, micropropagation, or layering.

The following points will give you a guide of what to look for:

The Grafted Plant

The first telltale sign that a plant is grafted is the price tag. It is quite usual for grafted plants to be double the price of a cutting-raised plant; the skill involved to produce them justifies the extra cost. When a magnolia has been grafted it is often because it is a plant that does not root easily from cuttings. The graft union on a plant two or three years old is clearly visible. After that it can become increasingly more difficult to see, especially when the chip budding method has been used. The way to tell at a later stage is that the older wood below the graft union is often a different shade of colour; and it is rougher and more fissured than the younger growth above. There can also be a noticeable change in thickness of growth near the base of the plant where the grafting has been carried out.

Even reputable nurseries can slip up. What often happens is that the graft fails and the rootstock grows unchecked. A nurseryman can easily overlook this during busy periods. To discover you have been growing the rootstock, perhaps for many years, is infuriating.

To add to the problem of detection, the leaves of the rootstock can look identical to the grafted

The Cutting-Raised Plant

Most magnolias are raised by this method and you cannot really go wrong. They are relatively cheap to buy, suckering is not a problem, and you are guaranteed a plant true to type.

The Seed-Raised Plant

Because seedling magnolias are the least expensive, the price makes them very tempting. I would never advise anyone to buy seed-raised plants of the large Asiatic magnolias, such as the species *M. campbellii*, *M. sargentiana*, *M. sprengeri* and *M. dawsoniana* unless you want to save the surprise and delights (or disappointments) of flowering for the next generation. If you are lucky they might flower in less than 15 years, on the other hand 30 – 40 years is not unheard of.

Since this is not a vegetative form of propagation one cannot be sure of the eventual flowering characteristics. The size, shape and colour may be inferior to what you would hope for. On the other hand, they might all be better than visualised. The bottom line is that it is a gamble, and do you want to wait to find out?

Many of the magnolia cultivars we grow are derived from chance seedlings, so we are very grateful to those who have had the patience to grow and select seed-raised plants in the past, to provide us with the wealth of treasures available today. If unlimited space is available, seedlings of the large Asiatics could be a viable proposition for planting en masse. But why buy them when you can collect seed from known superior forms and grow them yourself? It is far more rewarding (see Propagation, page 22).

Magnolia species which are frequently raised from seed are *M. kobus, M. salicifolia, M. sieboldii, M. wilsonii, M. sinensis, M. globosa* and *M. acuminata*. The early-flowering species are erratic in their seed production, which is dependent upon the temperature at the time of flowering; in favourable years they can produce seed with

plant, particularly if the same species has been used, making the differentiation between the named plant and its rootstock impossible. In this instance, if there are any growths that look suspicious, check that they come from above the graft union.

One other problem that can occur is that after several years a seemingly healthy plant can die for no apparent reason.

Usually this is attributed to something sinister like honey fungus, but close inspection of the roots may reveal that they are in perfect health, and if left the plant will start to shoot from the base. One theory is that an incompatibility between the rootstock and grafted growth occurs. This is very rare and should not deter anyone from purchasing a plant raised by this method.

A young grafted plant; the difference between the root stock and the growth of the new grafted plant is clearly visible. If it is a grafted plant that you are buying, always check the graft union. If you suspect that the graft failed, reject it

amazing abundance. Most of the later-flowering species are not affected by the spring frosts and usually set viable seed.

Many of the aforementioned species are difficult to propagate from cuttings, so raising them from seed is the most economic and practicable option. Again, being seed-raised there will be a subtle variation, but usually there is no alternative way to buy them other than grafted plants. If you are prepared to go further afield in pursuit of perfection there are many selected forms available; for instance, a nursery in Switzerland sells 19 different forms of *Magnolia*

sieboldii all of which are propagated vegetatively

Unlike the species *M. campbellii, M. sargentiana, M. sprengeri* and *M. dawsoniana*, many of the smaller-growing magnolias will start to flower at about five years from seed, which is quite acceptable.

Other seed-raised magnolias are sold at more specialist nurseries, which are geared for the enthusiast. These would include species such as *M. hypoleuca,*

M. officinalis 'Biloba', *M. tripetala, M. macrophylla, M. delavayi* and, very occasionally, *M. nitida*. All these plants are difficult, or seemingly impossible, to root from cuttings.

You can get a rough idea how healthy a plant is by looking at its growth. It is not so easy in the spring when the plant is dormant and has no leaves. It may of grown well the previous year, but since then it has had half a year to perish. The only sure way is to look at the roots. The plant on the left is how it should look. The plant on the right should be rejected

Plants Produced by Micropropagation

Plants produced by this method have been sold in Britain for over ten years, all of which have been propagated in America. The range of cultivars propagated by this method has been steadily increasing. There is no way of telling if a plant has been propagated by this method, nor will it usually indicate it on the label.

The following magnolias have been produced by micropropagation: *Magnolia acuminata* var. *subcordata* 'Miss Honeybee', 'Butterflies', 'Yellow Fever', 'Yellow Lantern', 'Betty', 'Wada's Memory', 'Galaxy' and several of the *M. grandiflora* cultivars including 'Edith Bogue', 'St. Mary', 'Victoria' and 'Hasse'.

In the future the majority of shrubs sold at garden centres might be produced in this way.

Dead or Alive?

It is worth bearing in mind two possible problems when buying plants in the spring.

1. During the winter freezing conditions can kill the roots. Keeping the plants in an unheated greenhouse or polytunnel is not sufficient protection during very cold periods. If the roots have been killed during a severe winter it is still possible for the plant to flower and come into leaf in the spring, only to collapse and perish soon afterwards. A plant is only as healthy as its root system. Ideally, it would be nice if plants were grown in transparent pots so you could see the condition of the roots. I dare not suggest that you invert the plants and take off the pots to inspect the root system before you buy, as it could make an awful mess, not to mention the verbal abuse you would get from the retailer. But on returning home, check that they are healthy and off-white in colour; if they are brown, return the plant immediately.

2. The majority of plants for sale in the spring have probably been grown in a protected environment, which would bring them into growth earlier than usual. When these plants are planted outside they are very vulnerable to frost damage. If you are diligent and are prepared to protect them well when frost is forecast, they can be planted immediately. However, it is far safer to keep them in a protected environment and to wait until all chance of late frosts have passed before planting them in the garden. Other points to look out for:

Selecting the right plant

The most fundamental mistake is buying a plant that is not suitable for its location. With the range of cultivars that are now available you are able to choose magnolias that will grow from 1m (3ft) to giants reaching 30m (100ft).

It is advisable for all the large-growing trees to be grown on a single stem; never buy a plant with two stems, as they are susceptible to splitting in strong winds. Some of the smaller-growing magnolias can be grown multi-trunked, with three or more stems; they not only look better but are also more stable.

Occasionally, garden centres sell *Magnolia stellata* that have been grown as standards (to look like giant lollipops) and recently I have seen *Magnolia x soulangeana* grown in the same way. Compared to some trees, magnolia bark is dull and uninspiring so why emphasise this fact? The style obviously appeals to some (or the standard rose would not exist) but be warned, whilst they might look nice in the garden centre, they would be very difficult to keep compact and tidy.

Check the health of the plant

There are only two serious insectivorous pests that you need to look out for: vine weevil and red spider mite (see Pests and Diseases, page 66). Leaves should look healthy, yellowing leaves are a sign that the plant could be pot-bound, starved of nutrition, water-stressed or has red spider mite.

The plant must be vigorous, look at the amount of growth it made during the previous season. Make sure that it still has a terminal bud, very often these can be accidentally knocked off. If this does happen, a new leader will grow from a bud lower down, but this can disfigure the plant for two or three years and will need to be trained with a cane to ensure the new growth stays as vertical as possible.

Ensure that the plant is well-rooted and stable in the compost. A young plant with a poor root system may never develop properly. Canes are used in pots to train plants, and to protect young grafts and vulnerable leaders from getting damaged by wind and human carelessness. However, they should not be used to prevent young plants from lying prostrate due to a poor root system.

Nearly all magnolias are sold in pots; the few exceptions are plants usually imported from Europe and root-balled in netting or burlap (an open-weave hessian sacking). The netting or burlap does not rot as easily as generally thought, and should always be removed carefully before planting.

Planting

If there is a secret to success, it is the initial planting or, to be more precise, the planting medium. It cannot be stressed enough how important the preparation of the planting area should be. All too often this is overlooked.

As you may have to put up with waiting a few years for a plant to flower, you can derive great pleasure and satisfaction in the interim period by seeing the plant growing well. A magnolia that struggles to put on a few centimetres of growth a year, when you need to wait until after adolescence before it flowers, can be very frustrating and demoralising.

Unless your soil conditions are perfect, which is most unlikely, the concept of simply digging a hole twice the size of the pot being sufficient preparation is futile practice. Other trees and shrubs may put up with that treatment, but where magnolias are concerned, time and effort at this stage will make all the difference.

Irrespective of whether the magnolia you are intending to plant is in a two-litre pot or a twenty-litre pot, the size of hole needs to be the same, particularly if your soil is not ideal.

Left: The thorough preparation of the ground is very important. The incorporation of well-rotted organic matter such as manure and leaf mould is vital

The Soil

The soil should be a deep loam with a high organic content, free-draining yet moisture- retentive and slightly acidic – this is Utopia and, for most, just a dream!

Fortunately, magnolias are tolerant of a wide range of different soil types, although a slightly acidic soil is preferable. The most suitable magnolias to grow on alkaline soils are: *Magnolia kobus, M. stellata, M. liliiflora, M. grandiflora*, the hybrids *Magnolia x loebneri* such as 'Leonard Messel' and the *Magnolia x soulangeana* cultivars. Other species tolerant of alkaline soils are *M. acuminata, M. delavayi, M. sinensis* and *M. wilsonii.*

Planting in a soil of a high pH (alkaline – over pH7) is the only time I would recommend the incorporation of peat in the preparation of the planting area. Sphagnum moss peat has a pH between 3.8 and 4.4. A cheap alternative is leaf mould, made from pine trees grown on an acidic soil. Both of these materials will counteract the alkalinity of the soil.

Magnolias are also tolerant of both dry and wet soils. *Magnolia virginiana* is native of the east coast of America. Its common names include swamp magnolia, swamp bay, swamp laurel and swamp sassafras. As one can guess, in its native habitat it is a plant of wet woodland, yet it grows perfectly well on dry, sandy soils.

When magnolias are planted on heavy soils, avoid walking or using machinery anywhere near the root system while the soil is wet. Once a soil of this type has been compacted, it is almost impossible to alleviate the problem without damaging the roots. For this reason, preparation of the ground for planting should be carried out during freezing conditions to allow wheeled access for bulky materials. The best time to prepare the area is during a dry spell in the winter. There

are three reasons for this:
1 Usually during the spring and summer there is not enough time to do the other 101 jobs that need to be done. And physical work such as digging is far more enjoyable on colder days.
2 If the area is prepared several months beforehand, the soil settles down and you do not end up with a plant in a sunken hole.
3 The organic matter that is incorporated into the planting area will absorb moisture during this wetter time of year, so if there

are dry spells during the spring and early summer, there is a reserve of moisture to keep the plant growing well.

Usually magnolias grow better when they are in a well-cultivated bed as opposed to being grown as a specimen in a lawn, and the preparation of the planting areas differs slightly (see page 46).

Above: A well sited plant with no competition from other plants. Allow plenty of room from the onset when planting a large growing magnolia such as this *Magnolia* 'Charles Raffill'

Siting

So often trees and shrubs are not given enough space to develop and show off their full beauty. Planting too closely at the outset is a bad policy; admittedly the larger the range of plants you have the greater the interest, but this interest is relatively short-lived. As the canopy becomes enclosed the plants will be drawn towards the light, the lower branches will die, smaller plants will weaken and perish and

all you will be left with are bare stems – not very inspiring!

Some magnolias have a heavy fragrance; others are more subtle and delicate. Make sure that they are accessible to the nose, not in the back of a border where this cannot be appreciated.

Sun
All magnolias will grow in full sun and some, especially *Magnolia grandiflora*, positively revel in it. Whilst they will also tolerate heavy shade, weak growth will be produced and they will be shy-flowering.

The smaller varieties must not be grown under a dense canopy; not only will they grow poorly, they need sun to illuminate the flowers for at least part of the day. This is particularly important with magnolias that have pendulous flowers which, when backlit by the sun, are exquisitely beautiful.

Wind

It is worth bearing in mind that sheltering trees from the prevailing wind may expose them to bitterly cold winds in the winter. The magnolia most prone to wind damage is the hybrid *Magnolia* x *veitchii*. It is the fastest and tallest growing one, which accounts for its susceptibility.

Wind is also a problem for magnolias with large leaves; *Magnolia macrophylla* is the worst affected. Unfortunately, it also requires protection from the cold wind during the winter; this is best achieved by the use of evergreen trees to act as wind breaks. The same applies to *Magnolia dealbata* and *M. rostrata*, although the leaves of the latter are not as huge, it is particularly tender.

It is a pleasure to see the leaves of *Magnolia macrophylla* developing into their huge dimensions, but they must be sheltered from strong winds

Cold

Most of us do not have a garden large enough to have areas with notorious frost pockets, you either live in one or you do not. But even small gardens have their own microclimates, depending on aspect, buildings and plantings in the vicinity.

Tender magnolias are best planted in a sunny aspect where the wood can harden up before the onset of winter. Be prepared to give protection during those vulnerable spring nights. However, plants grown in a sunny aspect are more prone to frost damage in the spring, as they will come into growth earlier. The evergreen species *M. grandiflora*, *M. delavayi* and *M. virginiana* var. *australis* are particularly susceptible to cold winds; the wind chill factor is far more devastating than the minimum night temperature, and in extreme cases plants can be totally defoliated.

Although it is not possible to grow some of the more tender species and their varieties other than in the mildest parts of the country, there is always a temptation for gardeners to grow the seemingly impossible. As new introductions are made from higher altitudes or more northern geographical ranges, coupled with the effect of global warming, there is an ever-increasing chance of success. Plant breeders are also assisting by hybridising tender magnolias with hardy forms.

When do I plant?

In theory, magnolias that are grown in pots can be planted at any time of year. However, having tried planting at different times and seen the consequences, I now restrict this to late spring, which coincides with when most are sold anyway.

Autumn was always the recommended time to plant, firstly because it is often a wet time of year so irrigation is not a problem, and secondly, the soil is still warm from the summer heat so the plant has time to root into the new soil before the onset of winter, giving it a head start in the spring. Although this seems plausible and is great for other plants, it has a drawback. Most pot-grown magnolias are kept undercover in ideal conditions, therefore they put on a lot of growth during the summer. This growth is not usually hardened off sufficiently for severe winter temperatures and could be damaged.

Planting in early or mid-spring seems the ideal period but, unless you live in the milder coastal areas of the country where late frosts are exceedingly rare, it is not to be recommended. Although very tempting, planting at this time can have disastrous consequences. A mild spell in early spring can start the flow of sap, then all that is needed is a sharp frost for a plant to be killed outright. In the spring of 1997 the severe late frost in the Home Counties not only killed young plants, but larger specimens also suffered severe die-back and bark split.

For most parts of the country, late spring is ideal. By then severe frosts are uncommon and the plant has time enough to put on good growth for the wood to harden before the onset of winter. The only disadvantage is that you will probably need to irrigate during dry spells. Do not irrigate from early autumn onwards, as this will encourage soft growth which again could succumb to frost damage.

Planting as a lawn specimen

Mark out a circle with a diameter of 2 m (6½ft); place some large plastic sheeting around the marked area. Cut away the turf to a depth of 5cm (2in) and place it on the sheeting. Remove the rest of the topsoil also on to the sheeting, anything from 4-40cm (1½in-1½ft). (There is usually a distinct difference between the topsoil and the subsoil, the former being darker in colour).

Dig out the subsoil on to the plastic, so that you end up with a hole approximately 1m (3ft) deep. This may seem excessive considering magnolias are surface-rooting but is important for two reasons. Firstly, it encourages the roots to grow downwards where moisture is more plentiful and secondly, for large-growing specimens, anchorage is improved, so making it less susceptible to being blown over. If it is possible to acquire good topsoil from elsewhere, remove all the subsoil from site, if not, keep the top half of the subsoil on the sheet and the rest can be disposed of.

You then need to incorporate plenty of organic matter into the remaining heaps of soil. A mixture of 60 per cent soil 40 per cent organic matter is an ideal proportion. The organic matter can be well-rotted leaf mould, manure (preferably horse manure, made with straw instead of wood shavings) and well-rotted garden compost which should be soil-like in texture and must not have had an alkaline accelerator added to quicken the decomposition.

A mixture of either the manure and leaf mould, or manure and garden compost in equal

A perfectly shaped specimen of *Magnolia sargentiana* var. *robusta* growing at Nymans Garden in Sussex. Having been given plenty of room to develop, and with no competition from other plants it has retained its lower branches

amounts, should be used with the soil. Although peat is also very good, try and avoid using it; apart from the cost, it is too valuable a resource to waste on planting, especially when the above mentioned are perfectly satisfactory. The only exception is when planting on soils with a high pH. Peat has a very low pH of 4.5 and this counteracts high alkalinity.

Start back-filling the hole by replacing the subsoil mix (or acquired topsoil mix). When the hole is half full put in the turf that was removed, then continue back-filling and finally finish off with the mixed topsoil. During the back-filling it is essential that after every 10cm (4in) of back-fill it is firmed well, otherwise the large amount of organic matter mixed in with the soil will in time decompose and the soil level will sink severely. This can be detrimental for two reasons: firstly, because it looks unsightly, so the tendency is to fill it in, raising the soil level around the stem which will cause premature death. Secondly, annual mulching will slowly raise the level of the surrounding soil, accentuating this problem over a period of time.

Ensure that when the planting has been completed the roots are only just below the surrounding grass level.

Planting in a cultivated bed

This gives you a greater opportunity to improve the condition of the surrounding area. The hole is prepared in the same way as planting in a lawn, but the surrounding soil should also have organic matter incorporated by trenching. The addition of this not only improves the fertility, but also creates a more 'open' soil structure, making it easier for the roots to travel in their search for nutrients.

For those who have a heavy clay soil, ensure when digging that the base of the hole is not compressed and sides are left roughened, so you do not create an impermeable barrier where water cannot penetrate. If the soil does get waterlogged extra drainage will be needed, or rotting of the roots is inevitable.

It is often recommended that a compound fertilizer should be incorporated into the soil when planting,

Magnolias grow better when planted within a border; they are easier to maintain and are not damaged by machinery such as mowers and strimmers

but as long as the correct organic matter is used, this is unnecessary.

When planting, if the roots are pot-bound and have started circling around the pot, these can be gently uncoiled. The roots are very fragile and are likely to break so extreme care is necessary. Because they are so brittle, all you can do is to open them out slightly. This will prevent them strangulating the other roots, which would lead to poor growth and instability. Make sure the plant is firmed in well. This usually means a bit of gentle footwork, even on small plants.

The most common mistake when planting is the incorrect level of the soil at the base of the plant. It is critical that the soil level only just covers the existing compost level, as even 1.5cm (½in) of soil covering the stem of a small plant could be detrimental. Conversely, no roots must be visible after planting. Check this particularly after watering in.

Aftercare

Staking

It is always advisable to stake small plants, as it helps stabilisation while new roots are being formed. It also makes the plant more visible to humans with big feet and to brainless dogs. Staking should be carried out while the roots can still be seen, so when a cane or stake is pushed in, the roots are not damaged.

If planting a pot-grown plant, avoid pushing stakes or canes through the compost ball. The stake must be placed on the outer edge of the compost, even if this means it is at a slight angle. After a couple of years the support is usually unnecessary. It is important to check the ties regularly to ensure they do not restrict and cut into the stem. This is also a common occurrence with plant labels, so if the label is around the base of the stem, always remove it and tie it onto one of the lateral branches.

Damage caused by plant labels and tree ties is very common, they are often overlooked and discovered too late

Shading

If the magnolia has been grown in a greenhouse, even one without shading, the leaves can be severely damaged when exposed to strong sunlight in the open. If planting in these conditions, it is important that the plant is lightly shaded until such time that it has become acclimatized.

Protect from rabbits and deer

Forget carrots, magnolias are the rabbit's ultimate delicacy! You can be assured that if you leave a plant unprotected for one night, it will be the night that they get a craving for one. Deer are even worse, your magnolia could be there one minute, and gone the next! (See Pests and Diseases, page 66.)

Watering

The need to water is obviously dependant upon weather conditions and the time of year. Watering the plant well immediately after planting helps to settle the soil around the roots.

Mulching

With hot, dry summers becoming more frequent mulching seems to be more important than ever. Mulching is beneficial for four reasons:
1 It prevents water loss from the soil.
2 It can have nutritional value.
3 It acts as a weed suppressant.
4 It looks aesthetically pleasing.

Mulching immediately after planting is very useful, as it is at this stage that the plants are most vulnerable to drought. The best material is well-decayed manure, ideally horse manure. Other mulches that could be used include leaf mould, well-rotted garden compost, pulverised bark and wood chips.

All manure must be well decayed and should not have a strong smell. Fresh manure has a high ammonium content, which can cause burning to the root system, and it also contains viable weed seeds. It is during the process of decomposition that heat is generated which kills the weed seeds in the manure.

The thickness of the mulch depends on the age of the plant. For young plants, up to 7cm (2¾in) can be used; for mature

The use
of tree tubes,
netting or
spiral tree
guards must
be used if
rabbits
could cause
damage

specimens, approximately 10cm (4in) is ideal. Never put any mulching material around the trunk. The uptake of nutrition is mainly from roots that are beyond the leaf canopy of the tree, not under the tree itself. Therefore ensure the mulch is spread over a wide area.

Do not use peat as a mulching material. Apart from being environmentally unethical, it is very difficult to wet after a dry period and forms an impenetrable layer, preventing any rain getting to the soil. For the same reason be careful using grass clippings that are not composted; if the layer gets too thick, it has the same effect.

Transplanting

Magnolias have a reputation for being difficult and fickle. Literature will tell you that disturbance to the roots can be fatal, so one would assume that digging a plant up and transplanting it is out of the question – this is not so!

Some reasons for transplanting could be:
• To move a plant that is in the wrong place.
• To replant because it refuses to grow (usually because it was badly planted in the first place).
• To take with you a plant of sentimental value when you move house.

Apart from the necessity of a water supply to irrigate the plant during the spring and summer, the limiting factor is the size of the root ball and the ability to lift it. Do not underestimate the weight, it is very deceptive. For this reason it is doubtful that a plant more than five years old can be moved without mechanical intervention, unless it is one with a small, bushy habit.

The best time to carry out this procedure is in late winter, just before plants break out of their winter dormancy. You will not encounter any taproots, but the root spread can be extensive. The fewer roots that are severed, the greater the success, so cut the roots as far away from the stem as possible. The chance of a 'small team' successfully lifting a root ball that is more than 1m (3ft) wide is unlikely without a visit to the chiropractor the following day.

If it is a large specimen that you intend to move, it is best if preparation starts the previous year. In late summer, carefully thin out the branches so that the roots have less growth to provide for. Removing the lower branches is useful, as it also makes it easier to work underneath the tree. The overall appearance, however, must not look 'butchered'.

Once you have decided how large the root ball can be, the removal of the plant is best carried out in the following way:

Cut around the plant to a spade depth.

Cut around the plant again one spade width beyond the first cut, and dig out this section leaving a trench around the plant.

Repeat this by cutting around the plant a third time and again dig out the trench, leaving a trench two spade widths wide. This is necessary to be able to dig underneath the plant. Depending on the size of the plant the trench may need to be considerably deeper.

Dig out a ramp where the plant can be lifted, or more likely dragged out. Start digging underneath the plant, leaving the root ball balancing on a shallow pinnacle of soil underneath.

With a large piece of strong sheeting, tightly roll half of it, and place the rolled end underneath the plant, opposite the prepared ramp.

A second person (whom you must not shout at if it goes wrong!) needs to lean the plant in the opposite direction of the ramp.

Dig underneath the plant utilising the extra space the ramped area gives you, to retrieve the rolled piece of sheeting, which can then be unrolled so it is underneath the root ball.

Summon assistance from the neighbourhood to assist you to lift or drag the plant up the ramp to its newly prepared site.

If the plant is large, to minimise disturbance cut the sheeting to remove.

Before replanting, cut cleanly any roots that may have been damaged. Once planted ensure watering is carried out before the soil has a chance to get dry.

If most of the soil falls off the roots in the process, only swear a little bit. It is also possible to transplant a bare-rooted magnolia as long as most of the roots are undamaged.

After the magnolia has been planted, if it is of any size it must be staked. Rather than drive a stake through the root ball, it is better to support the plant with guy wires, placing the pegs some distance from the plant. Ensure the plant is protected from the wire where it is in contact with the tree. This is achieved by threading the wire through short lengths of garden hose.

Out of necessity I have successfully moved ten-year-old plants which were up to 5m (16ft) high during a very hot spell in June. That would usually be a recipe for instantaneous death to most trees, and something I would never recommend. It was carried out in the following way:

The branches were thinned and half the foliage was removed. The remaining foliage and stems were sprayed with an anti-transpirant spray containing polyvinyl acetate. Shading covers were placed over each transplanted tree until the autumn, and intermittent misting was used on hot days. In total 20 plants were moved and all have survived and flourish. This demonstrates how resilient they can actually be.

Because transplanting will inevitably cause stress to the plant, this can result in an abundance of flower buds for the following spring. These are noticeable towards the end of the summer. They should be pinched out as soon as possible since the energy used to produce the flowers is best conserved for growth the following year.

When you suspect poor growth is the result of bad planting you have two choices. If the plant is small enough dig it up and start again in a correctly prepared area. Alternatively, you can excavate the surrounding area, back-filling it with enriched soil, as you would when planting.

Cultivation

As plantings mature, they must be periodically appraised, removing plants that are inferior before they begin to damage others nearby. This does not only refer to the top growth., but must also include the stump and as much of the root as possible. Anyone who has experienced the devastation that honey fungus can cause will understand why this effort is necessary.

When removing plants nearby, the last thing you want to do is damage the roots of the magnolia which will increase the chance of infection. If access by machinery is not possible, the removal of stumps is a lengthy process. Never cut a tree down to the ground and then decide to remove the stump. Leave as much of the trunk and crown as possible to give extra leverage and weight to pull it over. Portable winches are a great help to do this, assuming you have a suitable anchor point. The use of stump grinders may seem a good alternative to the hard work involved in digging a stump out, but they must not be used for two reasons:

1 Most stump grinders used in gardens only go down to a depth of 20cm (8in), which leaves an ideal host to allow honey fungus to spread, despite the stump not being visible.

2 As the wood decays, the soil covering will continue to sink for decades. This is particularly annoying if it is in an area of lawn.

Weed Control

Prevention is better than the cure. No job in the garden can be as demoralising as clearing a bed of weeds that have already dispersed their seeds. Try and remove them before this happens. Because magnolias are surface-rooting the use of a mulching material is more necessary than with most other plants. Mulching will suppress all but perennial weeds, eliminating the need to use forks, spades and hoes, which would inevitably cause damage to the root system.

Try and pull out any perennial weeds when the soil is damp. If re-growth appears the use of a weedkiller containing glyphosate is recommended. This is a translocated non-residual herbicide, with a low human toxicity.

Previous page: Mature plants of *Magnolia stellata* and its cultivar 'Water lily' growing amongst dwarf rhododendrons and conifers within the rhododendron species collection, Windsor Great Park

The chemical is absorbed into the weed and gives good results even with the most difficult perennial weeds. As with all horticultural chemicals follow the manufacturer's instructions carefully.

Residual weedkillers should not be used. The reaction of the chemical is very variable on the type and condition of soil. I have seen them used on light sandy soils with dire consequences.

Feeding

If the plant is mulched annually or biannually with well-rotted horse manure, there is no need for any supplementary feeding of fertilizers. It can actually be detrimental, for the following reasons:

• It can cause soft growth, which is susceptible to frost damage.

• Long extension growth can be weak and is likely to break.

• It can increase the time you need to wait for flowering.

• It encourages excessive vegetative growth so the amount of flowering growth produced is decreased.

If the plant is growing in an alkaline soil the leaves may become yellow due to the inability to produce chlorophyll. This condition is called chlorosis. In this instance it is due to a deficiency in iron, which can be cured by the application of iron chelate (sequesterine) which may need to be applied annually to counteract the alkalinity. Other reasons for chlorosis can be conditions which are too wet or too dry, attack by pests or low temperatures.

An application of a foliar feed can be beneficial to stimulate the plant to grow, particularly if it has been 'pot bound' before planting out. It is sometimes necessary to foliar feed the first year after planting while the plant adjusts to its new growing conditions. If it is not fed, it is common for magnolias not to grow the first year after planting. Avoid foliar feeding on bright sunny days as this can cause severe leaf scorch and plants grown under glass are particularly susceptible to this.

Irrigation

Magnolias luxuriate in having the combination of heat and adequate moisture. It is important to provide irrigation to the plant until it gets established. If a magnolia has been planted well to start with, once it is three to four years old there should be no need to irrigate, as established magnolias are remarkably drought-tolerant.

It is more advantageous to water well and less frequently. Watering little and often does not allow water to penetrate deep into the soil. If you are lucky enough to have your own water supply, the easiest method of irrigation is a sprinkler system. Unfortunately, most of us rely on a normal domestic water supply and the use of a sprinkler is a wasteful method of application.

Due to the increased demand and recent dry summers, the conservation of our water supply has become a major issue. I sometimes despair at the unnecessary use of treated mains water in gardens. Rainwater is much better for plants in general, especially for those which grow in 'hard water' areas. Gardeners must use water wisely and to look at ways to conserve it. Every garden should have facilities to store rainwater.

The use of a porous hose is becoming increasingly popular. This system uses water more efficiently than a sprinkler. Immediately after planting the hose can be placed in the soil to a depth of 10-20cm (4-8in) and 15-20cm (6-8in) away from the root ball and covered over with soil. The pipe must not be removed after the plant has become established, as it will damage the roots. If not used at the time of planting the hose can be laid on the surface of the soil and then covered with the mulch. The use of this system allows the water to penetrate deep into the soil with little loss from evaporation.

If dealing with individual plants, instead of using a hose it is better to pierce two or three small holes in the bottom of a container, placed beside the plant, and to fill this occasionally, allowing the water to seep out slowly. This prevents the soil being washed away from the roots and there is no 'run off', which often happens when the surface of the soil is dry. No irrigation should be applied after late summer, or soft growth will be produced which then will be susceptible to frost damage.

Hostas pictured here with *M. Sieboldii* are a suitable plant for growing under magnolias; they are shade tolerant, have a long season of interest, of easy cultivation and can be mulched heavily while they are dormant

Underplanting

As I have stressed before, magnolias should be clothed so they almost touch the ground. Underplanting is therefore not necessary, as you should not be able to see underneath them. If the magnolia branches have been lifted in the past, it is sensible to utilise the area for planting. Because of the depth of mulching that should be carried out, the shade and the competition for water and nutrients, the use of shrubs is not a feasible option. The use of herbaceous plants is also limited, as whatever is planted must be left to their own devices. They must not be invasive, or need dividing, must be tolerant of shade, require no cultivation of the soil, and must put up with an annual covering of mulch during early spring. Finally, if all that is not enough, they should ideally be of interest when the magnolia is not in flower. The range of plants is therefore limited but plants such as hostas, martagon lilies, ferns and early spring bulbs placed in small groups are ideal.

CULTIVATION

53

Pruning

Most magnolias will need pruning at some stage in their development; the only exception could be the compact forms like *Magnolia stellata*. Very often, if the plant is well cared for in its early years, the necessity for major corrective pruning at a later date will be minimised. Any major pruning is positively ugly; furthermore it can be detrimental to the wellbeing of the plant. It is therefore important to have good foresight into the development and ultimate stature of each plant in relation to its immediate environment.

Ask a child to draw a tree and you will end up with a stereotyped image; a tall thick trunk with a big, bushy crown. Through the generations we have learnt to perceive trees in this way. I think beech and oak trees look great grown in that fashion. The big difference is that they are not grown for their floral impact. The flowers of both are insignificant to say the least, being wind pollinated; not even insects find them particularly attractive.

Sadly, large Asiatic magnolias are often treated in the same way; having waited decades for them to bloom, all you see is the underside of the flower. The cause is quite simple – a lack of vision, and unfortunately this affliction is not restricted

to amateurs. Many a crooked neck has come about by spending a day looking at magnolia flowers poised on branches 15m (50ft) high. With the exception of training plants on walls and those that are grown in pots, the need to 'shape' a magnolia is not necessary. Pruning a magnolia to keep it within a restricted area is a never-ending battle; the more you prune the more it retaliates and grows.

Allow magnolias to be clothed to the ground, so the beauty of their individual flowers can be appreciated However, there are exceptions. Some forms of *Magnolia acuminata* have flowers that are so insignificant they are not worth seeing (or planting) anyway. *Magnolia wilsonii* and *M. sinensis* have pendulous flowers and *M. globosa* and *M. sieboldii* have flowers that are semi-pendulous. There is no advantage in having these plants clothed to the ground; pendulous flowers are best viewed from below.

Reasons to Prune

A double leader

Trees occasionally have a tendency to produce two terminal growths, or leaders. When this happens it is important to remove the least dominant one so the tree does not become forked. When mature this can be disastrous, as it can lead to one of them breaking off in a strong wind.

Previous page: *Magnolia* x *kewensis* grown to perfection at the Royal Botanic Gardens, Kew

Below: Unfortunately due to poor management when this tree was young its fate is certain. The fork has split once already, and the wound has callused over, but as the tree grows the branches will get heavier causing it to split in two

Crossing branches

These can rub together and cause weak growth, or eventual death. Remove all small branches that are crossing and all that might cross in the future. Large branches that have been crossed for many years are best left alone, as the wound caused by removing them can be more harmful than if they were left. Occasionally, old crossed branches naturally graft themselves together. When this happens they cannot be separated and should be left alone.

Water shoots

These are also known as epicormic growths and develop from buds that usually remain dormant under the bark. They are very vigorous shoots that come from the side branches and the trunks of established trees. They generally appear when large limbs are removed or damaged by wind, or there is a change in nutrient and

moisture levels. They are very disfiguring, and if left will cross other branches causing further damage. It is important to remove them as soon as possible. If not, large wounds will be made in the process and very often the problem will recur the following year. However, if the top of the plant has been damaged then one of these vigorous shoots can be selected to form a new leader.

Dead wood

Some branches will inevitably die, probably due to lack of light. The sooner the dead wood is removed the quicker the plant will callus and seal over the wound. Cut the dead wood as near to the live wood as possible, so that no snags are left.

Lifting

This term is used when the lower limbs or branches are removed. As branches get longer the weight of the wood forces the ends of the branches nearer the ground. All magnolias are best clothed to the ground but the branches must not touch the ground for the following reasons:

When it is windy, the branches will rub the ground, damaging their undersides. It is difficult to mow, weed and mulch under the tree.

The branches can root into the soil. The rooted branch will then grow vigorously spoiling the

overall appearance of the tree. This layering can affect the main plant by reducing its vigour.

Removal of flower bud on terminal growth

Some magnolias flower so prolifically that a flower bud forms on the ends of the terminal growth. These develop during the summer and by early autumn are quite visible. They should be removed as soon as they are seen. Below the flower bud there will be at least one growth bud, which will shoot as normal in the spring. If the flower bud is not removed the new growth will not develop as fast and will start to grow at an angle.

When to Prune

This is a controversial subject as ideas have differed in the past. It also depends on what is being pruned. Unless they are grown against walls, magnolias do not require any form of annual pruning. Wall-trained plants are treated differently, as they need a strict pruning regime to keep them within bounds.

Free-standing specimens

I consider mid-summer to be the perfect time for pruning for the following reasons:
During the winter months the branches do not hang as low as during the summer. This is due to the weight of the leaves, sap

Left: At least once a year, check to see if plants need any corrective pruning. Remove growths or branches before they cross. Several years have lapsed for this specimen, the crossed branches need removing urgently

and new growth, which make the branches heavier. Pruning during the summer gives a more realistic idea of how much you need to remove.

Pruning immediately after flowering, as advocated by some, can encourage vigorous new growth, which in unfavourable climates is susceptible to late spring frosts. Magnolias can 'bleed' severely when wounded during early spring. The bleeding impedes the healing of the wound, prevents the ability to apply a wound dressing and, at its worst, can be fatal to young plants. In mid-summer the flow of sap is minimal and no bleeding occurs.

Right: After the removal of large branches there is a tendency for plants to produce 'water shoots' from around the wound. If any large wounds have been removed check in late spring and summer to see if any new buds are forming, if so these can be rubbed off

Wall-trained Plants

Evergreen Plants
Magnolia grandiflora

This evergreen magnolia has been trained against walls for centuries. For them to flower at their best, they should be grown on a sunny wall. Very often *Magnolia grandiflora* is planted against a wall with the intention of keeping it trimmed, but it is soon left to its own devices, ending up as an unruly specimen that dominates the building. The sight of a well-kept specimen grown in

proportion to the building is in a class of its own.

The flower buds develop on the ends of the previous year's growth, and on short spurs on the current season's growth, which gives the long succession of bloom. This makes annual pruning difficult without the loss of flower. By mid-summer, all the flower buds that will open during that year are clearly visible. This enables you to carry out pruning without removing any of the flower buds for that year, but inevitably you may be cutting away shoots that will carry flower the following year. No annual pruning is necessary other than to keep it in shape, but cut back any growths that

grow directly out from the wall. If any drastic pruning is to be carried out, it is best to forfeit a year's flower and prune in early to mid-summer irrespective of any buds.

Magnolia delavayi

This species is also suitable for training against a wall as it makes an attractive foliage plant and can be pruned in early to mid-summer. Try to avoid growths that have flower buds on them, but if these are cut off it is not great loss, as you are not missing much anyway.

Above: A trained Magnolia grandiflora at Lanhydrock in Cornwall. The scent of the flowers is always appreciated near a house

Both species will need attention during late summer. Any long growths made during the year must be tied in to the wall to keep them in good shape and to protect them from wind and snow damage.

Deciduous Spring-Flowering Magnolias

For maximum effect it is important to have a tight framework of branches. Before planting, wires should be tightly secured across the wall at intervals of 15-20cm (6-8in). As the plant matures, the main framework should be self-supporting.

When the plant is young it will put on lots of growth, which is further stimulated by the pruning. This is not

conducive to good flowering. Unfortunately, it is not until the plant is of some considerable age that an abundance of flower buds will be produced, most of which will be on short woody spurs along the branches. When the plant is mature enough for this to happen, the effect is magnificent.

The flower buds for the following year are formed after the initial vigourous growth in the spring. Because of this, wall-trained magnolias are best pruned after the flower buds are visible, during late summer, as follows: Select the branches that are needed to continue the main framework. If the branch has no flower bud, cut back by at least half to a leaf bud, which will encourage a denser framework. Tie this onto the supporting wires. If a shoot you require for the framework has a flower bud, prune back by half immediately after flowering in the spring.

Cut all long non-flowering side growths made during the current season back to within 1cm (½in) of the main branching system, ideally leaving at least two buds from which the new growths will shoot the following spring.

When tying-in do not allow the branches to cross. Once the new leaders are tied-in, remove as many of the old ties as possible so that they are not left to cut into the stems.

What to Use

Using a saw

If it is necessary to remove branches with a saw, make sure that when the branch falls the bark does not tear beyond where you cut. The resulting wound can be very disfiguring and detrimental to the plant's health. Magnolias are prone to tearing so to ensure this does not happen proceed in the following way:

Remove the main part of the branch first by cutting underneath it, at a convenient distance from the trunk, to a depth of at least a quarter of the diameter, removing the saw before it is pinched.

Above: *Magnolia* x *soulangeana* 'Alba' looks very effective trained against a dark wall, although a strict training and pruning regime is required to keep it tidy

Left: An old and well maintained *Magnolia grandiflora* growing at Sutton Place in Surrey. No other evergreen plant has such a majestic and stately appearance

Make the second cut from the top at a distance approximately 10 cm (4in) out along the branch, parallel to the undercut. When this cut reaches the level of the first cut it will break cleanly along the grain without twisting or tearing.

For the third cut, take the weight of the section that is left in one hand and saw the remaining section off. Do not leave a snag; all branches must be cut flush to their source to prevent die-back.

Using Secateurs and Loppers

Magnolia wood is very soft and easily bruised; any bruised wood will be prone to die-back so it is important that the severance is made cleanly. For this reason I would not recommend secateurs with a flat-bedded anvil; the more expensive curved-anvil type are preferable. These are frequently used incorrectly; to achieve the cleanest and closest cut, the blade not the anvil must be nearest the finished surface. To avoid going around the plant in circles trying to achieve this, when cutting thin wood twist the secateurs in the hand and use them upside-down. Any cuts too thick for secateurs should be sawn and smoothed with a sharp knife. The use of loppers is inadvisable, as the cut is rough and they bruise the wood.

Wound Sealants / Protective Dressings

As the wood is very soft it is also prone to decay when exposed. The bark gives the wood a protective layer from fungal spores and harmful insects, which would otherwise attack the heartwood. All wounds over 3cm (1¼in) wide should be treated with a wound dressing. As the bark of magnolias is grey, the black colour of these compounds is disfiguring, but is a necessary evil. Large wounds must be retreated annually to ensure the wound is sealed. An alternative I find works well is lanolin, which being opaque in colour is not obtrusive.

Greenhouse
Pot Culture

Whether you need to grow seedlings, rootstocks for grafting or grafted plants and cuttings, the cultural requirements are the same.

Composts

All magnolias need to be grown in an acidic (ericaceous) compost, not in a multi-purpose compost. These composts are called multi-purpose as they have a fine particle structure with little nutrient so that they can be used for both inserting cuttings and potting, not because they have a dual purpose for both calcifuge and calcareous plants. It is the addition of magnesium limestone which makes these unsuitable for magnolias; the leaves can turn yellow within a month and the plant will subsequently die.

Professional growers are offered a range of perfect composts suitable for all stages of growth. One compost manufacturer can provide a choice of 120 different composts, which goes to show the exacting requirements the grower demands.

The amateur is not so fortunate. I have tried most of the ericaceous composts available, including peat-free alternatives, and none come up to the same standard. Generally they are too fine, break down rapidly and consolidate, leaving the compost devoid of air. For most amateurs growing a few plants in the greenhouse it will suffice, but for the more discerning who requires larger quantities it is well worth seeking out better quality composts.

Basic amateur ericaceous composts can be used for growing on young seedlings when they are pricked out from the seed trays. They only remain in this compost for three months, which is not enough time for the compost to break down, neither do they require a high nutrient level at this stage. Do not allow compost in bags to become wet during storage, as it will rapidly decompose and will no longer be of use for potting.

In 1998 a new ericaceous compost was introduced for the amateur market which contains a pesticide (imidacloprid) for the control of whitefly, greenfly, blackfly and vine weevil. It works both systemically and by contact with the insect. The control can last up to 100 days for sapsuckers and one year for vine weevil.

The incorporation of a wetting agent is very useful for peat-based composts. Peat can hold up to ten times its weight of water, but when dry it repels water like a duck's back. A wetting agent can increase the absorption rate of peat by up to 40 times.

Unless composts are purchased in bulk loads, professional growers usually add two other ingredients before they are used - controlled-release fertilizer and insecticide.

Below: Magnolias respond well when the use of a slow release fertilizer is incorporated into the potting compost, but always follow the recommended rates

Controlled-Release Fertilizer

These are small, rounded granules or consolidated lumps, either yellow-orange or blue in colour and coated with a biodegradable organic resin. Water vapour penetrates the resin coating and dissolves the water-soluble nutrients inside. These dissolved nutrients then gradually diffuse through into the compost. The rate of release is determined by the temperature, which is why they cannot be mixed with the compost in the bag, as it could thereby become toxic to the plant.

Depending on the type used and the temperature the plant is grown in, these controlled-release fertilizers can feed plants from between three to four and 32-42 months, depending on the length of time the plant will remain in the pot.

Insecticide

This is incorporated into the compost to prevent the establishment of vine weevil. It is a blue, spherical, polymer-based granule, which contains chlorpyrifos. It is quite noticeable in the compost, and is effective for up to two years. Without the use of an insecticide, the probability of suffering with vine weevil damage is very high. In

the past it has caused huge losses for growers of indoor pot plants and hardy nursery stock.

Mixing your own compost

It is difficult for amateurs to make compost that is comparable to the better professional-purpose made composts. It is not even practical for professional growers unless they use large amounts. However, if you do wish to make a suitable compost, the following mix can be made cheaply and easily and is quite adequate for home use.

One year old seedlings of *Magnolia macrophylla* starting their second year of growth. Seedlings are most vulnerable during their first winter, not usually from the cold, but during damp weather the soft growth is susceptible to fungal attack. Good ventilation and air circulation is important to prevent this happening

Ingredients

Peat

This constitutes 80 per cent of the mixture. Peat can vary enormously depending on what it is derived from. For potting composts it is preferable to use a medium to coarse-grade Irish sphagnum moss peat.

Perlite

This is a granular expanded volcanic rock. It is sterile, has a neutral pH and is available in four grades. It improves drainage and aeration, and retains moisture. The smaller particle size is more suitable for use in propagation, 3-6mm ($\frac{1}{8}$-$\frac{1}{4}$in) is ideal for potting composts. Adding 15 per cent Perlite to the peat will improve the porosity and aeration.

Lime-Free Potting Grit

The addition of 5 per cent grit is added for drainage but its weight also helps with the stability of the pot.

Other optional ingredients could include a polymer gel. This absorbs and stores water and it is beneficial if plants are to be watered by hand, or if they are left for periods when there is a possibility of drying out. Other ingredients would be the slow-release fertilizer and the insecticide mentioned previously, but the latter is not available to amateur growers.

If a slow-release fertilizer has not been added, the amount of nutrient in composts is very short term. Regular feeding once a month with a weak solution of liquid fertilizer suitable for acid-loving or ericaceous plants will be necessary. Do not feed plants after late summer as the plant must not put on too much soft growth before the onset of winter.

Because magnolias respond so well to correct growing conditions under protection, overfeeding can be a problem. If the plant becomes too lanky it will produce weak shoots. This is not a problem with small-growing shrubby plants, such as *Magnolia stellata*, as long as the terminal buds are removed every few weeks, making the shoots subdivide and producing a bushy plant. Once the correct shape has been attained the amount of feeding should be minimal or flower buds will not develop.

When a tree-type is grown too vigorously, it will produce a weak stem with no side branching, and you end up with a plant that is useless. The only remedy is to cut the weak stem almost to the ground, or above the union if grafted. A bud will shoot from the base, which then needs to be trained to form the new leader. If it is a grafted plant, make sure the new growth does not come from the rootstock.

Watering

The method used depends on various factors: the number of plants you have, size of the pot, the amount of attention you can give and, finally, cost.

No system can beat the individual attention that is given by hand watering, checking each plant in turn to determine their precise water requirement. If you have the dedication it can be very relaxing, even a time for peaceful contemplation. Unfortunately, not many of us are in that position and in reality it is more often rushed. When this is the case plants are overlooked and losses will occur.

Peat-based composts can become so dry that if you emptied a whole watering can over them it would have no effect whatsoever. When this is so the plants need to be immersed in a bucket of water for several minutes before the peat will absorb water again. In the worst scenario the leaves will wilt and become so crisp they will disintegrate when crushed. All may not be lost. If the whole plant is immersed in water overnight, it may start to shoot again within a few weeks. Magnolias can have surprising regenerative capabilities.

There are two systems that are easy and cheap to construct, which will assist watering. Both can be automated using a mini water computer sold at most garden centres. Having an automated system will not only save you time, but will give you the opportunity to leave plants for days on end. However, do not rely on them completely, as the consequences of a malfunction could be disastrous. These systems are:

Capillary Matting

Commercial growers of pot plants have used this method of watering for many years. For amateurs who grow large numbers

of plants, this is the best system. You are restricted to the size and design of the pots that are used. It is only suitable for plants that are grown in pots up to two litres, since if they are any larger the capillary rise is not sufficient. The pots must be flat-bottomed, so that the holes in the bottom of the pot are in contact with the matting.

The matting itself is made of glass-fibre, polypropylene or rayon, has a high water-holding capacity of up to 3.5 litres per sq m (6 pints per sq yd), and disperses the water evenly throughout the material. The capillary matting made for the amateur market works well to start with as it is impregnated with a wetting agent, but unfortunately after a while it loses its efficiency and uneven wetting occurs, so more careful management is then needed. As professional matting is only sold in 50m (165ft) lengths, this is unsuitable for most people.

To use the system, lay down a sheet of plastic on flat benching or even a smooth flat floor, then lay the capillary matting on the top of it. Then put in a water supply, which is best achieved using a porous hose laid on the matting at required intervals.

Drip Irrigation

This is the best method for watering larger pots. A header pipe is laid down a bench or floor, and from it thin tubing is laid to each pot and fixed with a clip. A nozzle is then placed in the thin tube allowing a small amount of water through. There are various types and sizes of nozzle depending on the amount of water required. This system needs to have a pressure regulator fitted and a filter to prevent the nozzles from blocking.

Growing Specimen Plants In Pots

I have derived great pleasure from growing magnolias in a greenhouse, where the scent of flowers is much more appreciated in a confined area. A conservatory or greenhouse also gives you the chance to grow the more tender species.

The following species are recommended:
• *Magnolia grandiflora*.
The dwarf cultivars of this species are the most suitable, they bloom throughout the summer with powerfully lemon-scented flowers, and the bold shining evergreen leaves add interest during the winter.
• *Magnolia nitida*
This requires greenhouse treatment in most parts of the British Isles. The flowers are pleasantly scented, but it is the foliage that is its greatest asset. As the new leaves develop in the spring they are bronzered, and the adult leaves are remarkably glossy. Being evergreen it is a superb foliage plant all-year-round.

Opposite: For those who live on very alkaline soils, you can still enjoy growing magnolias such as *Magnolia stellata* in containers

• *Magnolia coco*
A magnolia I have not seen outside a greenhouse. The small, white flowers are very fragrant but only open for a very short period. It has good evergreen foliage.
• *Magnolia virginiana*
The variety *M. v. australis* has attractive evergreen foliage and perfumed flowers, like a combination of lemon and a rose.
• *Magnolia stellata*
Because of its slow growth this is the only deciduous magnolia that is suitable for pot culture. Grown under protection it flowers at least a month earlier than normal with unblemished flowers, a delightful harbinger of spring. Some cultivars of *M. stellata* have no scent whatsoever. A cultivar like 'Water Lily' is ideal as it has attractive flowers and a lovely delicate scent. Pruning immediately after flowering is necessary to keep it compact.

Although I must not stray too much from magnolias, it is worth mentioning the genus *Michelia*, one of the more tender members of the magnolia family. In a greenhouse or conservatory the michelias make stunning plants and the smaller-growing species are well suited to pot culture.
• *Michelia figo*
This is slow growing, the flowers are either small, white and edged with purple (which are preferable)

or plum-coloured. The scent is reminiscent of very ripe pineapples mixed with peardrop sweets, admittedly not the most heavenly of perfumes, but different
• *Michelia champaca*
The most divine scent of any plant I have come across in the magnolia family. The flowers are lemon-yellow, pale orange or white, not conspicuous, but powerfully fragrant. It is from this plant that champac oil is derived, a celebrated perfume of the east. The plant must be kept in a heated greenhouse, which must not fall below 5°C (40°F) during the winter, but even at this temperature it may become deciduous.
• *Michelia doltsopa*
A fast-growing species, so would only be suitable for a large conservatory, but it has all you could wish for, with luscious, 15-25cm (6-10in) evergreen leaves and prolifically produced scented flowers in the spring. The flowers of the cultivar 'Silver Cloud' are larger and produced with greater profusion.

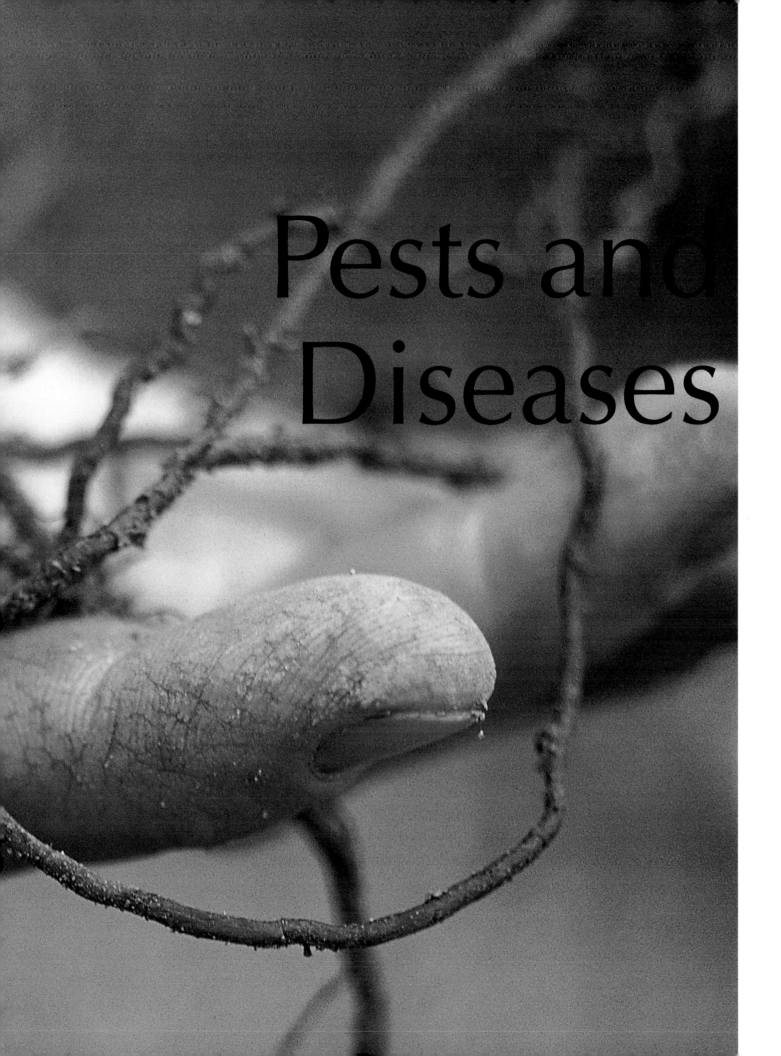

Pests and Diseases

Pests

VINE WEEVIL

This is a serious pest for a wide range of plants. The grubs are not choosy as to which roots they devour; favourites include fuchsia, cyclamen, primulas, strawberries and rhododendrons. Unfortunately magnolias are also susceptible, particularly those grown under glass.

The adult weevils are 8mm (½in) long, dull black with faint speckling, and can be seen from early spring to late summer. They are usually only active at night, as during the day they hide under leaves, pots and seed trays and only move if they have been disturbed. The grubs are 5-10mm (¼-½in) long, off-white with a light brown head and legless until fully grown.

The first sign in the spring is that the plant does not come into leaf, is loose in the pot and the compost on the surface is soft and fine-textured. Plants up to three years old can have the base of the stem girdled, which will be the same for all the roots. The plant at this stage is beyond saving. On examination of the compost one or more grubs may be found. These must be destroyed and the compost disposed of. Unlike other plants (especially rhododendrons) the adult weevils do little damage to magnolias, occasionally they will notch the margin of a leaf, but do nothing more serious.

Juvenile magnolias planted in the garden can also be killed by root damage caused by vine weevil. When planting, it is worth checking the pot compost for any signs of vine weevil activity. Look for any 'runs' that have been excavated by the grub; these usually travel down the side of the compost and the grub is often at the end of the run in a curled position.

Woodpecker damage is often seen on lime and oak trees, but it is occasionally found on magnolias. It does not seem to be detrimental to the health of the plant

Control

It helps to keep the growing area clean and tidy, removing any unnecessary items that may serve as a hiding place. The eradication of the adult is difficult, contact insecticides are of no use as the weevils are elusive. Systemic insecticides do not work either as the weevils seldom eat the leaves.

If grubs are noticeable in the compost it is advisable to remove as much of the compost as possible without damaging the roots and re-pot into fresh compost. If this is done during the summer the plant must be kept in a cool, moist atmosphere to help it become established.

The best method is to prevent the infestation of grubs. It is now possible to buy compost to which the manufacturer has added a pesticide which will stop any grubs developing. An alternative method is to use a parasitic nematode (*Heterorhabditis* or *Steinernema* species) which is specifically for vine weevil grubs. These are contained within a sponge, to which water is added and the plants are then drenched with the solution.

RED SPIDER MITE

These are not actually spiders, nor are they red, which is confusing. The mites are a translucent yellowish–green colour with two prominent black dots on their backs, and are just visible to the naked eye, but best seen with a hand lens. During hot weather they become very active and multiply rapidly. The mites can become a serious pest when magnolias are grown under protection. It is often said that they do not like damp conditions but I have known infestations in a fog house with a constant 98 per cent humidity, so keeping a greenhouse continuously damp does not prevent them from occurring. When the infestation is severe they can totally defoliate a plant within a few weeks, and if left unchecked will prevent any new growth developing, which can cause the plant to die.

They are most noticeable between midsummer and autumn. The first sign is areas on the upper surface of the leaf that appear bleached, or finely mottled with small white dots. This is caused when the mites pierce the underside of the leaf to extract the sap. The eggs are laid during early summer and are enclosed within a 'nest' of fine webbing. During the winter the adults turn orange-red and cluster together, very often around the leaf scar on the branches or in leaf axils, as if waiting for the new leaf to emerge. Other favourite haunts include bamboo-canes and in the crevices of woodwork.

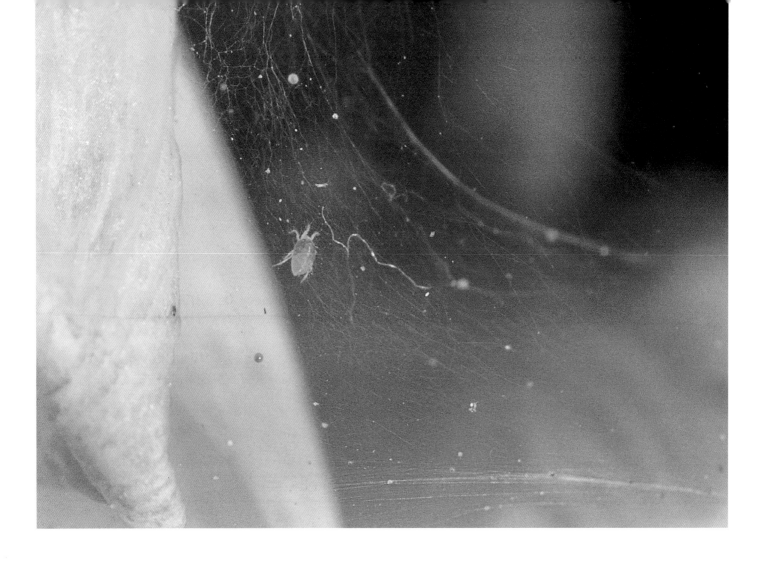

Control

The mites are difficult to eradicate; chemical control is possible, but you need to be persistent and thorough, particularly on the underside of the leaf and in the leaf axils. The web that covers the eggs and immature mites prevents the penetration of chemicals; therefore it is necessary to repeat the application several times to break their life cycle. The mites can build up a resistance if one type of chemical is used continuously; so a rotation of different chemicals is advisable to prevent this happening. The use of

tar oil before the leaves emerge will kill the over-wintering adults. An alternative to chemical control is the use of a sub-tropical predatory mite *Phytoseiulus*. Each one can destroy 20 immature or five mature red spider mites a day, and will lay 50-60 eggs during its life. Even the ferocious appetites of these predators can find it difficult to keep up with bad infestations, however.

If a magnolia is infected before it is planted outside, the red spider mites will continue to be active throughout the summer and defoliation can still occur.

The early detection of red spider mite is essential in order to achieve effective control. If the infestation becomes widespread it is very difficult to eradicate

WHITEFLY AND APHIDS

These pests only occur when magnolias are grown under cover and, apart from impairing the health of the plant, they are also very disfiguring. Their secretion is sticky and encourages sooty mould, which covers the lower leaves. This prevents photosynthesis, which in turn makes the leaves yellow.

Control

Both insects multiply at great speed so control is necessary at the first signs of infestation, and at frequent intervals, to be effective. Apart from the use of recommended insecticides which are readily available, biologi-

cal control for whitefly can also be successful, using a parasitic wasp known as *Encarsia formsoa*. These must be introduced at the first sign of a problem, as they do not eradicate an existing infestation.

Biological control of aphids can be achieved using *Aphidoletes aphidomyza*, a midge which lays its eggs next to the aphid colony and the larvae then feed on the aphids. Alternatively, the parasitic wasp *Aphidius colmani* also gives very effective control.

RABBITS

Being so widespread, they are one of the most destructive pests of magnolias. Rabbits are quite capable of stripping the bark off the base of the trunk, totally girdling even mature specimens, which will cause the plant to die.

Control

If rabbits are a problem in your area some form of protection such as wire netting or tree guards will be necessary from the outset.

DEER

Usually they just strip the tops, which can re-grow, but occasionally they can finish the job off, damaging the plants beyond recovery. In some areas the population of roe deer is increasing dramatically.

Control

Tree guards suitable for deer must be used if they could be a problem, or there will be disastrous consequences.

SLUGS AND SNAILS

Slugs can be a major problem to young magnolias. They eat the leaves with epicurean delight, which is clearly visible, but what is more serious and not so noticeable is that they are capable of eating a layer of bark around the base of the stem, killing the plant. This occurs with seedlings that are up to two years old. If left unchecked, they can wipe out a whole batch with great ease.

Young magnolias in the garden are also susceptible, particularly during prolonged periods of wet weather. Plants up to four years old can be totally

defoliated, and although the plants are too old to be damaged at the base, they attack the younger wood nearer the top of the plant. Tree tubes that are used to protect plants from rabbits and deer are an ideal environment for slugs and snails, so extra vigilance is needed to check for damage when they are used.

Control

Slug pellets containing metaldehyde or methiocarb are very effective, but if accessible to children or pets an alternative method of control should be used. A less toxic bait is now available, containing aluminium sulphate.

Above: Slugs and snails can totally defoliate young plants, but it is the removal of the young bark that can be a serious problem

Right: Do not underestimate the damage that rabbits can cause, even mature plants can be girdled and killed during the winter

Opposite: Wire or tough plastic netting is one of the best ways to prevent damage from rabbits

Diseases

HONEY FUNGUS (*ARMILLARIA*)

It is usually thought that this fungus only attacks damaged plants, or plants that are in poor health. This is not true, as healthy plants can also be killed. As an experiment I planted a healthy, vigorous magnolia in an area where I knew honey fungus occurred. The plant grew well, putting on nearly 1m (3ft) of growth for two years; the third spring it flowered well, but at the end of May I noticed the leaves were flagging, and on inspection found it was totally rotten at the base; it had succumbed.

It is now known that there are different types of honey fungus, some of which seem totally harmless. Unfortunately, in appearance they are very similar and it is not possible to identify the differences without sophisticated equipment.

The toadstools, as the name suggests, are honey-coloured and are most abundant during the summer and autumn. The decomposing fungi have an awful foetid smell. The fruiting bodies themselves do no harm apart from spreading the spores. It is the underground

Right: A young magnolia infected with honey fungus. When the strip of dead bark is removed, the white fans of pathogenic fungus will be seen underneath

Below: The toadstools of honey fungus appear in late summer and autumn. The presence of them in a lawn is usually an indication that there is decaying wood below the surface

It is often assumed that if a plant becomes infected with honey fungus fatality is inevitable; however, it is possible to save young plants as long as it is detected in time.

threads, known as rhizomorphs, which attack the plants. The rhizomorphs can be mistaken for dead roots of plants; they have a faint smell of fungus when rubbed between thumb and forefinger and are very tough to break.

Control

During the growing season, if the leaves of a plant start to turn yellow, the base of the stem should be examined. Check if there are any black threads coming from the soil and travelling up the surface of the bark. If there are, they

Below: Honey fungus is also known as 'bootlace fungus' after the tough black threads that travel below the soil's surface

must be carefully peeled off, removing as much as possible from the soil. The stem and the surrounding soil should then be drenched with cresylic acid. If the plant is not too large, foliar feed throughout the summer at three-week intervals to help it recover.

In areas where honey fungus is known to be a problem it is advisable to periodically check the base of all magnolias (and other plants) before any symptoms occur.

When a magnolia is badly infected, the bark will start to die at the base, moving up the trunk in narrow bands. Underneath the dead bark a white fan-like mould is visible. Even at this late stage, I have known plants to fully recover.

The dead bark should be carefully removed and the wound drenched with

cresylic acid. After this has dried the exposed wood should be painted with fungicidal tree paint. The callus on either side of the wound may start to grow, and in time the wound will seal completely. If the bark at the base has been totally girdled it is too late; the plant must be dug up and burnt.

When using cresylic acid ensure all the manufacturer's safety procedures are followed. One thing the manufacturers do not inform you about is that after treating the soil, your garden will smell of a public convenience for several weeks!

Directory

Species and Their Cultivars

Magnolia acuminata
Cucumber Tree

Native of eastern North America, it is the most widely distributed of the American species. This is a fast-growing, deciduous tree of easy cultivation and will grow into a large, stately tree up to 25m (80ft) in height. Its botanical name refers to the shape of its leaves, which are acuminate - long and pointed at the tip.

It is the only magnolia that has disappointed me twice. I did not become acquainted with this species until after seeing the more flamboyant Asiatic magnolias. The small greenish-yellow, claw-shaped flowers appear in early summer, at a time when the new foliage is lush and nearly fully expanded.

If this tree were precocious, like many of its Chinese relations, the floral impact would be

noticeable. Unfortunately, flowering when it does, you could be forgiven if you walked underneath a tree in full flower and did not notice it. The flowers stay erect for two days, but instead of opening out as you would expect, the tepals fall off.

The flowers have a faint scent, which is not disagreeable, nor particularly pleasant.

After being disappointed with the flower, I could not wait to see the spectacular seedpods, to which the common name refers. In the autumn I was told that a tree at Waterers Nursery in Surrey was laden with

Previous page: The largest and most spectacular specimen of *Magnolia denudata* I know grows in the warm climate of Ticino, Switzerland. It is estimated to be between 150 and 175 years old

Above: Although the flowers of *Magnolia acuminata* are not the most beautiful, the species has been invaluable for its breeding potential

seedpods, so off I went excitedly, camera in hand. I first noticed small, dull-red seedpods on the ground underneath the tree, which were no more than 5cm (2in) long. I assumed they had not been fertilised and had aborted. Looking then at the seedpods on the tree, it was evident that was not the case.

If it is not for its ornamental value, why is this species grown? The North American Indians had a good use, to hollow out the trunk to make canoes. Another use has been to use seedlings as rootstocks for grafting, but it is not renowned for producing large quantities of seed.

However, it does have a great horticultural value in its breeding potential; firstly, because of its hardiness and secondly, for the yellow pigmentation of the flower. It is one of the hardiest species of magnolia; laboratory tests have shown that one-year-old shoots can withstand temperatures of -35°C (-31°F). Its yellow coloration is also unique within the genus, and it has been hybridised with other species to produce some exceptionally beautiful and hardy magnolias, such as 'Elizabeth', 'Butterflies' and the *M. x brooklynensis* hybrids.

Cultivars
'Golden Glow'
Discovered in Tennessee in 1957. The flowers are pale yellow and not long lasting and are concealed by the large light green leaves. It starts to flower at four years of age.

'Koban Dori'
(Golden Plate Bird)
Bright yellow flowers, very prolific from a young age. Originally from Nakamura, Japan. Probably the best of the Magnolia acuminata cultivars.

'Large Yellow'
Large pale yellow flowers which are produced on young plants.

Magnolia acuminata var. subcordata

This variety was once known as *Magnolia cordata*, but is now considered a variety of *Magnolia acuminata*. It is native to the south-eastern United States and because of its more southerly distribution, it is not quite as hardy. The plant is noticeably pubescent and slower growing with pale yellow flowers. The name refers to its leaves, which are cordate at the base (two well-defined lobes, one either side of the petiole).

Cultivars
'Ellen'
Unusual as it has a variegated leaf, worth growing if you like these.
'Miss Honeybee'
Light-yellow flowers on a young plant, young leaves very pubescent on underside.

Magnolia amoena

A deciduous tree native to China. The flowers are small, pink and fragrant. This magnolia was only introduced to Britain in 1990 and to date has not flowered here. The specific name means delightful, so it holds promise for the future.

Magnolia biondii

A deciduous species native of China, it was introduced to Britain around 1987. In 1908 Wilson sent seeds of this species to the Arnold Arboretum of Harvard University, but they failed to germinate. It closely resembles *Magnolia salicifolia* in both leaf and flower. The flowers are small and start to open in early spring and have a good scent; a mixture of lemons and freesias. It has not been in cultivation long enough in Britain to evaluate its full ornamental potential.

Magnolia campbellii
Campbell's Magnolia
It is native of eastern Nepal eastwards through Sikkim, Bhutan, Assam and Yunnan. Because of such a wide geographical range there is great variation within the species.

Joseph Hooker collected the species in 1849 at a time when it was one of the more common trees and whole mountainsides were covered with it. Like so many plants, its numbers have been drastically diminished due to the demand for firewood and timber.

Plants of this species raised from seed can take a long time before they start to flower, 20-25 years is not uncommon, although grafted plants of named cultivars will flower in 12-15 years.

The flowers have an upright poise on leafless branches in the spring. I have seen plants in Cornwall start to flower in mid-January, but more typically they flower from March to April. Unfortunately, this does render them liable to frost damage.

Above: The yellow flower of *Magnolia acuminata* 'Koban Dori' is a great improvement on the type of species

Right: The flowers of *Magnolia biondii* are small and attractive, they are not produced with abundance on young plants

Trees in cultivation should grow rapidly in their early years, but as the plant ages the growth rate slows. Trees can become almost as wide as they are high, ultimately reaching 15-20m (50-60ft) in height.

The flowers are up to 25cm (10in) wide and vary in colour from pure white to deep cerise; typically the outer tepals open flat whilst the inner tepals remain closed giving a 'cup-and-saucer' effect. A mature plant in full flower can appear like a cloud in the sky and must rate as one of the most magnificent floral displays in the plant kingdom.

Cultivars
'Betty Jessel'

This is a seedling raised by Sir George Jessel in 1937 from Magnolia campbellii 'Darjeeling' which grew at the Lloyd Botanical Garden, Darjeeling, India. The flowers are dark purple-crimson and are usually cup-shaped. The centre of the flower is flushed white, giving a bi-coloured effect. The original seedling took 23 years to flower, but grafted plants can start flowering from five to seven years of age. It is the last Magnolia camp-

The shade of colour of *Magnolia campbellii* flowers are variable, it is best to buy known cultivars

bellii to flower, usually during mid-spring, giving it a greater chance of escaping frost damage. I consider this cultivar to be one of the finest magnolias I know.

'Darjeeling'

Similar in appearance to 'Betty Jessel' and almost as gorgeous, but the white flush on the inside of the flower is not as prominent. It first flowered at Hillier's Arboretum in 1974.

'Landicla'

Very large flowers, deep pink at first fading to pale pink as the flower ages.

'Queen Caroline'

A cultivar grown at The Royal Botanic Gardens, Kew. Attractive, deep pink flowers, but not too exciting; it may have been better as a younger plant.

'Wakehurst'

Vibrant redish-pink colour, a flower that stands out amongst the crowds.

Magnolia campbellii var. *alba*

The original white form still grows at Caerhays Castle, Cornwall and was raised from seed sent from Darjeeling in 1926. From a distance the flowers appear pure white, but all the white forms I have seen have a pink or occasionally green coloration at the base of the flower. When raised from seed it flowers at an earlier age than the type. The original plant flowered when 14 years old. The leaves are also longer, and more attractive, than the type.

Cultivars
'Caerhays Clone'

This is the cultivar that was awarded the F.C.C by The Royal Horticultural Society in 1951, and was the first white form to be introduced to Britain. A beautiful flower 25cm (10in) across with purple staining at the base and very large leaves.

'Ethel Hillier'

Large, white flowers with a hint of pink at the centre on the underside. The flowers seem to be particularly frost-tender.

'Strybing White'

Large, white flowers 30cm (1ft) wide, the outer tepals hang down, so not the most elegant of flowers but they are produced from seven years of age. It has the largest and most attractive leaves of any precocious-flowering Asiatic species which measure up to 43cm (1½ft) long.

Above:
Magnolia campbellii var. *mollicomata* 'Lanarth' has the darkest flowers of any *M. campbellii* cultivar

Left:
Magnolia campbellii var. *alba* is not as common in cultivation as the pink form. Seedlings of this variety have produced some outstanding plants

Magnolia campbellii var. *mollicomata*

This was introduced by George Forrest in 1904 and comes from the more eastern range of the species. It differs from the type species in many ways; most noticeable are the fine hairs (pubescence) on the flower stalk, and the shape of the flower, the inner tepals retaining a bulbous appearance. The flowers open slightly later and it begins to flower at an earlier age from seed, usually 12-15 years. The colour of the flower is very variable and ranges from almost pure white to a deep cerise-purple.

Cultivars
'Lanarth'

The seed was collected in Yunnan by George Forrest in 1924; it first flowered in 1947. The colour of the young flower is deep magenta, unlike any other magnolia. As the flower opens it gradually fades

to a deep purple-violet. The plant has several distinctive characteristics; it has an erect habit and the flower buds are the most pubescent I know. The pubescence also covers the flower stalk and the ends of the branches. It is the least hardy of all the M. campbellii group. Only plants raised vegetatively can be given this cultivar name, as its seedlings can vary from the true type.

'Werrington'

This was raised from the same seed collection as 'Lanarth'. The flowers are slightly paler, and it is reputed to be hardier.

Magnolia cylindrica

This deciduous species was named by E H Wilson in 1927, but was discovered by one of his collectors. It did not reach Britain until 1950. Unfortunately, the plant we grow in cultivation does not correspond to how Wilson described it, and therefore is considered by many to be a hybrid.

The specific name refers to the cylindrical seedpods that the species has, and when compared to seedpods of the plant cultivated as *M. cylindrica*, the difference is very apparent. Some authorities consider the cultivated plant to be a hybrid with *Magnolia denudata*, as they are found in the same province of China. However, the plant that has been grown and is still being sold as *Magnolia cylindrica* is the more ornamental of the two.

When mature, there is no other magnolia that is so distinguishable by its growth habit. The branches are typically layered, slowly making a large shrub or small tree as wide as it is high. The flowers, which open on naked branches in mid-spring, are white with a faint rose flush at the base, and sit erectly from the spurs along the branches.

Magnolia dawsoniana
Dawson's Magnolia

This magnolia was discovered by E H Wilson on his third Chinese expedition in 1908 and was named in honour of Jackson T Dawson, who was the first superintendent of the Arnold Arboretum, Boston.

Opposite: *Magnolia cylindrica* is a beautiful species from China

Right: *Magnolia dawsoniana* 'Valley Splendour' is a named form that grows in the Valley Gardens in Windsor Great Park

This deciduous species will grow into a medium to large tree. The flowers are not as large, nor as spectacular, as the other large-growing Asiatic species, but it does have great charm. The flowers on mature specimens are produced in great abundance, so the overall effect is still quite showy. The slightly fragrant, pink flowers, open in early spring. They seem to weigh the thin branches down, causing the tepals to flop which gives an untidy appearance to individual blooms. The leaves are obovate, very thick and dark green, dissimilar to any other large species. Grafted plants start to flower from 8 years of age; seedlings will take at least double the time.

Cultivars
'Clarke'

This form is superb, and in a class of its own. The flowers are larger than usual, rich pink on the outside, paler within; they have two whorls of tepals, which are most noticeable when the flower is fully open, the inner ones being shorter. Flowers from 6 years of age. Originated at Clarke Nursery, California.

Magnolia delavayi

Another Chinese magnolia introduced by E H Wilson in 1889; the first specimen was collected three years earlier by a French missionary, Pere Jean Delavay, after whom the species was named.

It is the leaves, not the flowers, of this species which are the main ornamental attraction. The thick, leathery, evergreen leaves are matt-green and can be over 30cm (1ft) long. It grows rapidly into a dense, multi-stemmed plant, attaining tree-like proportions in favoured climates. The flowers are fragrant, creamy-white and short-lived, being at their peak at night, which is not a great asset.

This species is too tender for the colder parts of Britain and even in the Home Counties can be killed during harsh winters. In the milder regions of the country and those near the south and west coasts, it makes an impressive tropical-looking specimen. It grows well on alkaline soils, as demonstrated by the large specimen growing at Highdown in Sussex.

Magnolia denudata
Yulan, Lily Tree, Naked Magnolia

This was the first Asiatic magnolia, introduced in 1780. The specific name refers to the plant being denuded of leaves when it flowers, which must have been an unusual occurrence when it was introduced. Given a favourable spring, it must rate as one of the most beautiful species, the flowers being simple, elegant, and with an almost virginal quality. It is understandable why Buddhist monks have grown it to adorn their temples for nearly 1,500 years, which possibly makes it the first flowering tree to be used ornamentally.

Opposite: Pictured is *Magnolia dawsoniana* 'Chyverton' which makes a great display but no dawsoniana can match the superior quality of the cultivar 'Clarke'

Right: *Magnolia denudata* was the first Asiatic magnolia to be introduced to Britain, and is still one of the most beautiful

Above: The individual flowers of *Magnolia delavayi* are very attractive, but are only seen at their best in the early morning or in the evening

The ivory-white flowers open in early spring and have a rich, sweet perfume, but are easily damaged by spring frosts. The plant makes a large shrub or a small rounded tree, and is hardy in all parts of Britain. It is ideal for training on walls because the growth is of moderate vigour and a wall offers the flowers some frost protection.

Magnolia fraseri
Fraser's Magnolia, Ear-leaved Umbrella Tree

Introduced to Britain from America in 1786, it is native to the southern Appalachian Mountains. This is a fast-growing deciduous tree and grows to 20m (60ft) or more. It starts to flower in early summer and continues sporadically for several weeks. The flowers are white, with a pleasant scent. The leaves are up to 30cm (1ft) long, the flowers are half that size. Because the foliage hides the flowers, and most of them would be too high in the tree to appreciate the scent anyway, I consider the plant has little ornamental value, and hardly warrants cultivation.

Magnolia globosa
Globe-Flowered Magnolia

Native of the Himalayas from Sikkim to Yunnan; there are two distinct forms, the Indian and the Chinese. Forrest first introduced the less hardy species in 1919 from Tibet. The Indian form was introduced from Sikkim around 1930, and is the one more generally cultivated.

Left: The individual flowers of *Magnolia fraseri* are very attractive but are usually hidden by the foliage

Right: *Magnolia globosa* is one of the less common species from China

It is a deciduous shrub or small tree. The leaves are 18cm (7in) long and dark green. As they emerge in the spring they are covered with an attractive rusty-coloured pubescence, also covering the young growths, making it distinct from any other magnolia. The flowers, which are relatively small, appear in late spring and continue to come out through early summer. Unfortunately, the buds and flowers have a habit of going brown when damp, and even in perfect conditions they do not open fully, which I find disappointing. For this reason, I would grow *Magnolia sieboldii*, *Magnolia wilsonii* or *Magnolia sinensis* in preference.

Magnolia grandiflora
Southern Magnolia

It is native from Florida to North Carolina in the U.S.A. This magnolia must surely be the most magnificent broad-leaved evergreen plant that can be grown outside in Britain. It has been in cultivation here for over 250 years and specimens of 18m (56ft) are not uncommon, but plants grown in the open are very slow, getting as wide as they are tall. In warmer climates, such as along the Riviera and Italy, they can grow to enormous dimensions in a very short time.

The flowers start to come out in mid-summer and continue until the first frosts of autumn. The scent, which is rich and fruity, is one of the strongest of any plant that can be grown without protection in Britain.

Over 100 cultivars have been selected in America, which shows the diversity within the species.

Cultivars
'Anne Pickard'
A sport of Magnolia 'St George'. The yellow-variegated leaves burn in the sun, and have a tendency to revert back to green. It is not quite as awful as some of the variegated forms of *Aucuba japonica*, but not far off it. A plant of weak constitution and, fortunately, quite rare.
'Baby Doll'
A very slow and upright form, which grows no more than 15cm (6in) a year. Strongly scented, small flowers.
'Blackwell'
Very dark green, glossy foliage with undulating edges. It has a compact habit, flowers at an exceptionally early age and over a long period. It is remarkably hardy. One of the best cultivars for general planting.
'Edith Bogue'
A vigorous plant with narrow, dark green leaves. Very hardy.

'Exmouth'
It must be one of the most expensive magnolias ever sold. The original plant was grown in the garden of Sir John Colliton at Exmouth and in 1768 was one of the few sizeable specimens in the country; most of the young plants were killed in the severe winter of 1739-1740. The tree is reputed to have been rented out to nurserymen who sold layers at five guineas each. It is the most widely cultivated form in Britain. It has an upright, vigorous, straggly habit. The leaves are long, narrow, very often pale green and chlorotic. Nowadays there are far superior cultivars to choose from.
'Ferruginea'
A compact, upright habit. The leaves are deep green and very glossy, the underside is covered with a rusty-brown felting. Large, highly fragrant flowers.
'Goliath'
It has a very dense habit and has unmistakable mid- to dark green oval leaves with an undulated surface. When fully open the flowers are 30cm (1ft) across with a heavy fragrance. Selected at a nursery in Guernsey, Channel Islands around 1910.

The attractive evergreen leaves, long flowering period and the strong fragrance has made *Magnolia grandiflora* a popular choice for planting near a house

'Harold Poole'
First imported to Britain in 1986 from Louisiana Nursery in America. It is a compact plant of slow growth. It has beautiful, narrow, strap-like foliage, which is smooth, glossy and mid-green in colour. Flowers are produced after six years of age and are of average size. The good habit and distinctive foliage makes it very desirable.
'Little Gem'
A popular, hardy, dwarf cultivar growing 2m (6ft) in 12 years. The leaves are deep green, very glossy with a light brown indumentum and are up to 15cm (6in) in length. The flowers are small and cup-shaped and develop on the end of long flower stalks, which can be up to 6cm (2¼in) long. It does not bloom with profusion at a young age, but when it matures flowers are produced with abundance and continue for a very long period.

'Russet'
A very hardy, compact and slow-growing selection. The ends of the branches, buds and undersides of the leaves are covered with a fox-red indumentum. The flowers are up to 20cm (8in) across and have a fruity fragrance.
'Samuel Sommer'
A very fast-growing plant with large, glossy leaves. The richly scented flowers are up to 30cm (1ft) across, although young specimens can produce flowers of staggering dimensions. The widest I have measured was 43cm (1½ft) which is the largest of any Magnolia grandiflora. It is slightly tender when young.
'Victoria'
One of the hardiest cultivars available. Selected in Victoria, British Columbia. It has dark green, lustrous foliage with prominent brown indumentum on the underside.

Magnolia hypoleuca
Japanese White-Bark Magnolia

In the past there has been much confusion with the naming of this plant. It is still referred to in many gardens as *Magnolia obovata*, which is now an invalid name, or as *Magnolia officinalis*, which is a closely related species.

Magnolia hypoleuca comes from the primeval forests of the Japanese islands. The timber has great economic value and has been used extensively, which has seriously depleted the wild population.

The deciduous leaves are up to 46cm (1½ft) long and a light, fresh-green in colour and, unlike *Magnolia officinalis*, have a red-purple colouration on the petioles. The flowers are 23cm (9in) wide and start to open in early

summer and continue to come out for up to six weeks. They are off-white, occasionally with a pink colouration on the outermost tepals. They have showy bright red stamens which make them highly attractive. The scent of the flowers is so strong that if you smell one at close range it can be offensive, yet from a distance it is quite exotic and fruity. On a warm day, with the wind in the right direction, a tree in full flower can be smelt at a distance of 100m (330ft).

The cone-like seed pods are sometimes produced in abundance; they are large, bright red and have very distinct curved spines surrounding them. The foliage, flowers and seedpods are all attractive, making it a highly desirable large tree.

Left:
Magnolia hypoleuca is a vigorous growing tree which has very attractive highly scented flowers

Below: The individual flowers of *Magnolia kobus* are not spectacular but flowers can be produced in great quantity

Magnolia kobus

Native of forests of Japan and the nearby Quelpaert Island of South Korea, it makes a small to medium-sized deciduous tree. The flowers appear in the early spring, are small, white and have a delicate perfume. While they are not particularly glamorous, when the tree is in full flower, it has an air of simple beauty to it.

This is a very cold-hardy plant, suitable for exposed positions. Because of its wide distribution, plants of *Magnolia kobus* vary considerably; some have

flowers so small that they are not of great merit. As most of the plants sold are raised from seed, there is no way of knowing what you will get.

Cultivars
'Killerton'

A compact plant which flowers at a young age. The flowers are almost twice the size of the species. Unfortunately, it is seldom sold.

Magnolia liliiflora
Woody Orchid,
Lily-Flowered Magnolia

It was introduced to Britain from Japan in 1790 but is probably native to China although it is not known in the wild. It grows into a dense thicket and rarely exceeds 2.5m (8ft) in height.

It begins to flower in mid-spring as the leaves start to emerge, but is at its peak in late spring and continues for two months, although it is not so effective when the foliage conceals the flowers. It is useful in filling a gap, flowering between the precocious and early summer species.

Cultivars
'Holland Red'

Large deep red-purple flowers with a spicy fragrance.

'Lyons'

Long, upright, deep-purple flowers that are slightly distorted.

'Mini Mouse'

This must be the smallest magnolia. Despite my plant being grafted onto Magnolia kobus, which I would assume would give it vigour, it only grows 5cm (2in) a year. The leaves are 5cm (2in) long,

Magnolia liliiflora 'Nigra' has a long flowering period and often escapes the frosts in spring

and are thick and shiny, giving them an evergreen appearance. The flowers are disappointing. They are 2.5cm (1in) long, dull purple and are not produced in great numbers. It has little ornamental value and is only worth growing as a novelty.

'Nigra'

This is assumed to be the cultivar most widely grown, but much confusion exists regarding the identity of the true plant.

It should be of a more compact habit than the species with larger, deeper coloured flowers; often the darker flowers can be almost white inside, which contradicts the original description made by Veitch in 1861.

Magnolia macrophylla
Big Leaf Magnolia

Although introduced from SE America 200 years ago, this magnolia is seldom seen in our gardens. The specific name is made up of two words, macro = big and phylla = leaf. They are certainly the largest deciduous leaves of any tree that can be grown in Britain.

When the leaves first emerge in the spring they are fresh-green and paper-thin, standing erect on the branches and looking stunning with the sun shining through them. When fully grown they can be up to 1m (3ft) long and 36cm (1¼ft) wide, the upper surface being matt-green and the underside silvery-white.

It is not just the leaves that are stunning, the flowers, too, are magnificent and, like the leaves, are huge, measuring 36cm (1¼ft) across. They open in early to mid-summer and are white with a purple base and a lovely fresh fragrance.

The plant makes an open-branched tree rarely reaching 10m (33ft) in height. It is important not to grow it in dense shade, as the tree will be drawn up. Try to retain its lower branches so that the magnificent flowers can be seen close to.

This tree can be a little tender in its first few years, so protecting it during the winter is advisable. Because of its immense leaves it should be situated in a very sheltered position. The wood will harden up for the winter if grown in full sun, but the leaf size will be reduced. It is a remarkable architectural plant which gives a very tropical effect - guaranteed to cause comment.

Cultivars
'Gwavas'

A cultivar from New Zealand, which does not seem to have exceptionally large leaves, and although ten years of age it has still not flowered.

'Sara Gladney'

It does not have the purple blotch at the base of the tepals. Flowers over a long period.

'Whopper'

Flowers are multi-tepaled and reputed to be up to 48cm (1¾ft) across, although I have not seen one that size in Britain as yet.

Magnolia macrophylla has huge flowers to match the leaves, and never fails to impress

Magnolia macrophylla var. *ashei*
Ashe's Magnolia

It is smaller than the type in every respect and has a shrubby habit. Because of this the flowers can be more appreciated, particularly their strong, rose-like fragrance. This variety flowers at a very young age, three years is not uncommon. A very desirable plant, which unfortunately is now almost extinct in the wild.

Cultivars

I do not know of any named cultivars at present, but hybrids do exist between *Magnolia macrophylla* and its variety *M. m. ashei*.

Magnolia macrophylla var. *dealbata*

Considering it comes from Mexico, it grows surprisingly well in some Cornish gardens. It is the only deciduous magnolia that comes from the tropics. It has very good foliage, comparable to the type species, although I consider the flower to be inferior. Until recently it was considered a species in its own right.

Magnolia nitida
Glossy Magnolia

This species is native of S.W. China and S.E. Tibet and was introduced by George Forrest in 1917. It is frustrating that such a beautiful plant as this is not hardy and cultivation is restricted to the mildest parts of the country. Because of its tenderness it is rarely seen, but in Cornwall it will grow into a small tree.

It has the most sumptuous, glossy, evergreen leaves, but is particularly attractive just after the new bronzed-red leaves emerge in the spring. The creamy, scented flowers appear in late spring and early summer. It seems hard to propagate this magnolia from cuttings; fortunately it does germinate readily from seed when obtainable.

Magnolia officinalis

It was introduced by Ernest Wilson in 1900. This large tree magnolia has been cultivated in China for hundreds of years because of its medicinal properties, in which the bark, flower buds and leaves are used. A decoction is reputed to be beneficial for many ailments and is used as a tonic, a treatment for coughs and colds, and as an aphrodisiac. Because of the high medicinal value, most of the trees in the wild have been destroyed.

In growth and habit it is similar to *Magnolia hypoleuca*, with which it is often confused. The 20cm (8in) parchment-coloured flowers appear in early and mid-summer and are concealed by the large leaves. Their scent, which is very powerful, verges on being unpleasant, and at close quarters is actually completely disagreeable.

Cultivars
'Biloba'

A plant that has interesting, large, bi-lobed leaves. The flower is strongly scented, but not of outstanding beauty.

Magnolia rostrata

This deciduous tree is native of China, India and Myanmar. It is too tender for general cultivation in Britain, but in favoured locations it grows to 12m (40ft). Its foliage is very beautiful, particularly during early summer when the new leaves are bronze, quite unlike any other tree I know. Individual leaves can reach 50cm (1¾ft) in length and are very thick and dark green. The flowers that open in early summer are less spectacular; they are white and measure 20cm (8in) across and smell of over-ripe melons. Because of its simple flower and unique, bold foliage, to me it looks more prehistoric than any other magnolia.

Above: A flower of *Magnolia officinalis*, the similar flowered bi-lobed leaf form 'Biloba' is the more ornamental tree

Left: *Magnolia nitida* growing in the gardens of Caerhays Castle in Cornwall. This species has attractive flowers and stunning foliage

Magnolia salicifolia Japanese Willow-Leaved Magnolia

It was introduced at the beginning of this century from Japan. The specific name refers to the similarity of the leaves to a willow tree, the botanical name for which is *Salix*. When crushed, the twigs, leaves and bark have the most distinctive and pungent scent of any magnolia, being described as lemon or anise.

It grows into a medium-sized tree, with thin twigs, and is very hardy. The small, fragrant, pure white flowers are borne on young plants and open in mid-sprng. Individually they are not impressive, but when seen *en masse* are very effective.

Cultivars
'Jermyns'

A slow-growing, shrubby form that has larger leaves. The flowers have longer, thinner tepals, which I find less appealing.

'van Veen'

An upright tree with flowers that are very fragrant; the leaves are narrower than usual, having a graceful bamboo-like appearance.

Above: The colour of the flowers of *Magnolia sargentiana* var. *robusta* can vary from deep pink to pure white depending on the clone. This pale pink form grows at Nymans in Sussex

Right: *Magnolia sargentiana* var. *robusta* 'Multipetal' is unique and exceptionally beautiful

Magnolia sargentiana

Introduced from China in 1908 by Ernest Wilson, it is one of the four precocious, large-flowered Asiatic species. It most closely resembles *Magnolia dawsoniana*, but the flowers are larger, up to 20cm (8in) wide, and usually a brighter vivid pink, similar to that of *Magnolia campbellii*, which from a distance it can also be confused with. The leaves are dark red when young, which is a particularly distinctive feature.

It has a tall, slender habit and is best grown away from other trees so that lower branches can develop. It is not often cultivated in British gardens, but when a mature plant in full flower is encountered, its beauty is comparable with any other Asiatic species.

Magnolia sargentiana var. robusta

This variety differs in having flowers that are up to 30cm (1ft) wide, with much broader tepals, and they do not hang as horizontally. It has a denser, broader habit, and flowers at a younger age. The colour of the flower varies from white to light purple, but none has the pink flowers of the type species.

Cultivars
'Blood Moon'

The original tree grows at Strybing Arboretum in San Francisco. It has heavily scented, large, pale purple flowers. The stamens of many magnolia flowers are beautifully coloured, but the ones on this cultivar are so attractive it would be worth growing even if it did not have tepals.

'Multipetal'

Because the flowers have up to 27 tepals, they make the flower so heavy that they hang upside-down. This is unique and stunningly beautiful.

Magnolia sinensis
Chinese Oyama Magnolia

Introduced from China in 1908 by Wilson. This deciduous, large spreading shrub or small tree is the largest growing of the four related species (*M. sieboldii*, *M. globosa* and *M. wilsonii*). The flowers appear at the end of late spring, but are at their peak in early summer. They are the largest of the group, totally pendulous, fragrant and can measure up to 13cm (5¼in) across.

This species can be confused with *Magnolia wilsonii*, the main difference being that the latter has flowers that are smaller at 10cm (4in), the leaves are slightly smaller and narrower, and the new shoots are covered in a brown, rather than fair, pubescence.

Some years it can be laden with red seedpods which can be an attractive feature during the latter part of the summer.

Magnolia sinensis thrives in a diversity of soil types and is best planted where the flowers can be seen from below.

Magnolia sieboldii
Oyama Magnolia

It is native of Japan, Korea and China and, because of this wide distribution, there are subtle changes within the species, the most important being the colour of its stamens. The plants from Korea and the neighbouring part of China have stamens that are darker red in colour. Some plants of this species in cultivation have stamens that are light pink and are not so ornamental.

This magnolia must rate as the most desirable early summer-flowering species of them all. It is slow-growing, forming a large spreading shrub, producing flowers when very young. The flowers are pure white, with a lemony scent, and are semi-pendulous, so inviting you to see the attractive boss of stamens within. They start opening in late spring, and continue through to the beginning of mid-summer. Although it flowers after the leaves have developed, the foliage, far from concealing the flower, acts as a fresh-green foil. An exquisite magnolia for any garden, and particularly suitable for those of smaller size.

Left: The semi-pendulous flowers of *Magnolia sieboldii* show off the contrasting bright red boss of stamen in the centre of the flower

Below: The paper-white lemon scented flowers of *Magnolia sinensis* are pendulous, and are best viewed from below

Cultivars
'Genesis'

A colchicine-induced plant (see *Magnolia stellata* 'Norman Gould'), which has made everything bigger except the flower, which I find disappointing.

There are a number of other cultivars available, many with double flowers; none of them are much of an improvement on the typical species.

DIRECTORY

91

Magnolia sprengeri

Native to China and introduced by Wilson in 1901. A deciduous, large tree with flowers similar to *Magnolia campbellii*, but the flowers of *M. sprengeri* do not have prominent inner tepals that stand up. They are simply cupped in shape and the flower is smaller. The flowers are always pink, but vary in their intensity. What this species lacks in size of flower it makes up with its charm and brilliance of colour, making this species one of the most beautiful.

Cultivars
'Burncoose Purple'

It has a very fastigiate habit. The flowers are larger than the type and deep pink-purple.

'Claret Cup'

The flowers are saucer-shaped, rosy-pink on the outside, almost white on the inside.

'Copeland Court'

Originally a seedling from a Magnolia sprengeri at Trewithen. A beautiful flower of such a rich pink it seems to glow, even on wet, overcast days.

'Diva'

This was raised from seed sent by Ernest Wilson. The plant was grown at Caerhays Castle and was first thought to be a pink form of Magnolia denudata, but it soon became apparent this was not the case. It flowers very freely. The fragrant, clear pink flowers face every direction other than straight down and the ends of the tepals often reflex upwards.

'Eric Savill'

The colour of the flower is unique among magnolias. The underside of the flower is bright magenta and, when illuminated by the sun, becomes luminous. All is not perfect though; on closer inspection the tepals are crinkled, often deformed. When viewed from a

Right: There is more than one clone of *M. Stellata* 'Water Lily'. This highly attractive form is one of the best magnolias for small gardens and tubs

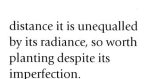

distance it is unequalled by its radiance, so worth planting despite its imperfection.

'Lanhydrock'

This is one of the many magnificent magnolias grown at Lanhydrock in Cornwall. Viewing the magnolias from the distant parkland surrounding the garden, this is the most noticeable because of its distinct dark colour. It originated as a seedling from the garden at Trewithen, was planted in 1969 as a five-year-old seedling and first flowered in 1980. The flowers are rich, dark pink, up to 20cm (8in) across.

'Marwood Spring'

The original seedling grows in Dr Smart's garden at Marwood in Devon and is now 30 years old. It is a third generation seedling. The seed came from a plant that was grown by the late Norman H. Haddon at Underway, near Porlock in Somerset, who grew his plant from seed that was collected off the original Magnolia sprengeri 'Diva' at Caerhays Castle in Cornwall. The flowers are very dark, and

similar to those of 'Lanhydrock'. The original seedling at Marwood started to flower at approximately 15 years of age; it would be assumed that grafted plants would start to flower from 10 years of age.

'Wakehurst'

Very similar to 'Diva' but the flowers are very slightly darker.

Magnolia sprengeri var. *elongata*

This variety has a white flower with a purple base. It is not as fast-growing and flowers at an earlier age than the type species. I was disappointed with it the first time I saw a young plant in flower; since then I have seen mature plants and my opinion has not changed. Compared to some of the cultivars of the type species, I consider it an ugly sister.

Left: *Magnolia sprengeri* 'Wakehurst' is one of the many excellent forms of this species

Magnolia stellata
Star Magnolia

The origins of this plant are highly confused, and while some doubt that it is a Japanese plant of wild origin, others consider it a hybrid between *Magnolia kobus* and *Magnolia salicifolia*. Whatever its origins, it remains one of the most beautiful and popular of all magnolias.

Because it is common and we are so familiar with it, its exquisite charm is often overlooked. It is a shame that the flowers are so easily blemished by spring frosts as it is one of the hardiest and most wind-tolerant, due to its low, dense habit and small leaf size.

Within the species the colour, number and length of tepals are variable, as is the delicate fragrance, which is occasionally absent. There are many selected cultivars available.

Cultivars
'Centennial'

Compact-growing and extremely floriferous. The white flowers have up to 30 tepals, which have a pink stripe up the back of them. Probably the best white Magnolia stellata available.

'Chrysanthemiflora'

A selection from Japan with small, pink, scentless flowers that have 30 tepals.

'Jane Platt'

I consider this without doubt the best pink

Left:
Magnolia stellata 'Jane Platt' is almost perfect; the only quality it lacks is a fragrance. It has only recently become available from specialist nurseries

Below: A beetle on its way to fertilise the flower of a *Magnolia tripetala*. Beetles are still the main pollinators of magnolias. The inner tepals remain closed for several days to give them a sheltered environment

Magnolia stellata available. Similar to 'Chrysanthemiflora', but the flower is slightly larger and the overall appearance not so rounded. The tepals are dark pink on the outside, pale within. The only fault is that they do not have a scent.

'Norman Gould'

This cultivar was created at the Royal Horticultural Society's garden at Wisley in the early 1950s. It is a genetically-altered *Magnolia stellata*. This was achieved by inducing the growing meristem with a highly poisonous alkaloid extract called colchicine, which doubles the number of chromosomes.

Colchicine is derived from *Colchicum autumnale*, the autumn crocus (which is not related to a true crocus). This magnolia is a slow-growing and squat plant, becoming as wide as it is high. The flowers are pure white and up to 10cm (4in) wide, and produced in abundance on the leaf-less branches during early spring. The flowers seem more frost- hardy than the typical species.

'Rosea'

Pink in bud, flowers pink with up to 14 tepals, which fade to white as they age. Very open habit.

'Scented Silver

This is a seedling of *Magnolia stellata* 'Green Star' raised by Dr. Frank Gaylon in the U.S.A. For a plant registered as a culti-var of *M. stellata* it has a very vigorous habit. The plant at Hascombe Court was grafted in 1989 and is now over 5m (15ft) high. This demonstrates that plants grown from stellata seed can produce plants more typical of *Magnolia kobus*. The large pure white flowers have the strongest fragrance of any magnolia within the stellata/kobus range.

'Water Lily'

Beautifully scented white flowers with more tepals than usual, the ends of which reflex upwards. It is slow-growing and has a dense habit, eventually reaching 3m (10ft) in height.

Magnolia tripetala
The Umbrella Magnolia

This deciduous species is found throughout the southern Appalachians in America and has been in cultivation in Britain for over 200 years. Its common name refers to its large leaves that radiate from the ends of the branches. It is a handsome foliage tree, growing to 10m (33ft), of easy cultivation and is very hardy. It has attractive seedpods which are bright red and 8cm (3¼in) long. The flowers appear in early

summer and are creamy-white, 20cm (8in) wide, although most of the time the tepals remain erect.

Now for the bad news: beetles are the main pollinators of magnolias; those that pollinate this species must be very closely related to the dung beetle. Unlike any other magnolia, the flowers of this species have a putrid stench, definitely not one for the vase on the dinning room table. This species is only worth growing if you have a warped sense of humour, and enjoy the look on the face of your unwary guests as they smell the flower.

Cultivars
'Bloomfield'
Much larger leaves than the type, and the flower is slightly larger. An interesting plant when viewed from a distance.

Magnolia virginiana
Sweet Bay
It is native of America and covers a long geographical range from Massachusetts down to Florida. It has been grown in Britain for over 300 years, which is longer than any other magnolia.

In Britain it grows very slowly, eventually reaching 10m (33ft) in height. Plants from the more northern range are much hardier and are deciduous during the winter. Plants from its southerly range are evergreen and less hardy. These have been considered distinct enough for them to be classed as a variety within the species known as *M. v.* var. *australis*.

The flowers start to open in early summer and continue to come out sporadically until late summer. They are 10cm (4in) wide when fully open, creamy-white, occasionally very pale yellow and deliciously scented. The fragrance does vary from plant to plant, some being lemon-scented, whilst others are more like a rose. The flowers do not make a great floral impact from a

Although the flower of Magnolia wilsonii *is smaller than* M. sinensis*, it can have the added bonus of butter yellow autumn colour*

distance and only open fully in the afternoon. It is a very versatile plant, growing well in full sun and in dappled shade. It can be a free-standing bushy tree or trained against a wall. Unfortunately it rarely sets fertile seed in Britain. For a plant with so many attributes it is a shame it is not easily obtainable from nurseries.

Cultivars
'Opelousas'
Deciduous slow-growing plant with large leaves. The flowers are 10cm (4in) across.

Magnolia virginiana
var. *australis*
This is the southerly type, which retains its leaves during the winter. Whilst this is considered the better form, during a harsh winter the leaves can become bedraggled, to a point that you wish they had fallen off anyway. It is therefore better to grow this variety in a sheltered position. The leaves on the upper surface are a matt-green and on the underside silvery-white, which is attractive when blown in the wind.

It seems to be slightly more vigorous than the type when young, but still maturing to the same height, unlike plants in its homeland which can grow to 28m (90ft).

Cultivars
'Henry Hicks'
The evergreen leaves are mid-green and up to 15cm (6in) long, with a silver underside. The stamens in the flower are very pale.

Magnolia wilsonii
This species was named after its collector who discovered it in China in 1904. It is vary similar in appearance to *Magnolia sinensis*, but with slightly smaller flowers. These are pure white, fragrant and pendulous and start opening in late spring, are at their peak in early summer, and occasionally have a fleeting second flush during late summer.

It is smaller-growing than *Magnolia sinensis* and may be trained to form a single trunk, the crown becoming conical in shape. It is easily distinguished in the winter by its brown-purple twigs. It is one of the few magnolias that can have a display of autumn colour, the leaves turning butter-yellow, but this does not occur every year.

Magnolia zenii
This species is a recent introduction from China, where it is very rare. It is a deciduous plant and has white, scented flowers with purple staining at the base, which appear in early spring. I first flowered it in 1990, four years after grafting. The disappointingly small flowers are 10cm (4in) across, and are of dubious merit. It is still too early to evaluate its full ornamental potential; some selections of this species may prove it to be worthy of cultivation.

Hybrids

'Albatross'
M. cylindrica x
(M. x veitchii 'Peter Veitch')
A seedling raised at
Trewithen in Cornwall,
and given to the Head
Gardener, Peter Borlase at
Lanhydrock in 1974. The
seed came from a *Magnolia
cylindrica* which is
assumed to have been
pollinated by a nearby
Magnolia x veitchii
'Peter Veitch'.

The flowers are up to
25cm (10in) across, look
white from a distance, but
have a pink flush at the
base. It flowers in mid-
spring before the leaves
appear. It starts to flower
at five years of age and will
become a small to
medium sized tree.

'Ann'
M. liliiflora 'Nigra'
x *M. stellata*
One of the 'Eight Little
Girls' raised at the United
States National Arboretum
during the 1950's. The oth-
ers are: 'Judy', 'Randy',
'Ricki', 'Betty', 'Jane',
'Pinkie' and 'Susan'.

I have often evaluated
them when grown together
as a collection, to choose
which ones are worthy of
cultivation. They are of
similar appearance and
their floral impact changes
from year to year depend-
ing on the season. They
look their best after a cold
spring, when the leaves
have not developed, and
perform better in a colder
climate, which they toler-

Right: 'Ann
Rosse' has
unattractive
flower buds,
but when
in full flower
it is very
desirable

Below: 'Ann'
like all the
'Little Girls'
gives a vari-
able floral
impact.
Some years
it can be
good, but
generally
I do not get
too exited
about them

ate very well. In time they
will all grow into densely
branched, small trees.

Suffice it to say, I do not
grow any of them, as per-
sonally I prefer their parents. However, my views
are not shared by all; six
of them (namely; 'Ann',
'Betty', 'Jane', 'Pinkie',
'Ricki' and 'Susan') have
all been given coveted
awards by the Royal
Horticultural Society.
Several nurseries sell them;
therefore I have included a
brief description of each.

'Ann' has red-purple
flowers, which stand very
erect on the branches.
It flowers earlier than the
other cultivars, starting in
mid-spring, so it can put
on a reasonable display
of colour before the
leaves appear.

'Ann Rosse'
M. denudata x
M. sargentiana var. *robusta*
This cultivar has such
unattractive, dirty-
coloured flower buds, they
do not hold much promise
for the flower, but nothing
could be further from
the truth because, when
open, they are extremely
beautiful. The 20cm (8in)
fragrant flowers are pale
pink on the outside, and
almost pure white within,
with a faint pink blush in
the centre. What really sets
it off are the bright red
stamens in the centre,
which gives the flower
a greater depth.

It was raised in 1963 at Nymans in Sussex from seed of *Magnolia denudata*. The original plant is no longer the most elegant of specimens, but young plants have a moderate rate of growth and will become a small to medium sized tree.

'Apollo'

M. campbellii var. *mollicomata* 'Lanarth' x *M. liliiflora* 'Nigra' hybrid ? One of the many excellent hybrids raised by Felix Jury in New Zealand. The flowers are up to 23cm (9in) wide. The tepals are violet-pink on the outside, pale pink to white inside and have very dark stamens. It will eventually grow to be a medium sized tree. The original seedling apparently flowered at two years of age, which is quite amazing.

'Athene'

'Mark Jury' x (*M. x soulangeana* 'Lennei Alba') The Jury family in New Zealand have raised many fabulous magnolia hybrids, which were introduced to Britain during the 1980s. It would be difficult to choose a favourite because they are all of exceptional quality, but this could be the one. It really has class, the fragrant flowers are very thick textured, up to 30cm (1ft) wide, ivory-white with a pink flush at the base on the outside, almost pure white within, and have an upright poise on the leafless branches.

It flowers at only three years of age, so initially the flowers are totally out of proportion to the size of plant and have to be seen to be believed. It is a vigorous grower, putting on up to 1m (3ft) of growth a year; so tempting as it may be, it is not ideal for the small garden.

'Atlas'

'Mark Jury' x (*M. x soulangeana* 'Lennei Alba') A Jury hybrid with flowers of immense proportions, which continue to fascinate me every spring. I enjoy looking at the reaction from people who stare upon the open flower with astonishment. The blooms are probably the largest of any Asiatic magnolia hybrid, but what makes it more astounding is, like the other Jury hybrids, it starts to flower at only three years of age.

The flowers are up to 36cm (1¼ft) across, pink on the outside and white inside, so when the flowers open fully the white insides of the lower tepals contrast well with the upright inner tepals.

This plant will become a medium sized tree, so plenty of space is needed; it must also be planted in a sheltered position to stop the flowers being damaged by strong winds.

'Betty'

M. liliiflora 'Nigra'
x *M. stellata* 'Rosea'
One of the more interesting of the 'Little Girls' from the U.S. National Arboretum. It has purple flowers with 12-19 tepals, which are white on the insides. It is at its peak during mid-spring, and will continue for a month. (See 'Ann', page 95.)

'Black Tulip'

M. 'Vulcan' x *M.* 'Iolanthe'
A hybrid raised by Mark Jury in New Zealand and released in 1998. It was selected out of 150 seedlings that were grown from this cross. The colour of the flower is unique; it is an exceptionally dark ruby-red.

No doubt this magnolia will be very sought-after when it first appears on the market. Attempts are being made to micro-propagate it in Britain, but as yet there has been limited success. The foliage is dark green and the new leaves are noticeably pubescent to the touch on both the upper and lower surfaces. It grows vigorously and will become a slender, upright, medium sized tree, which will flower from a young age.

M.x brooklynensis

M. acuminata x *M. liliiflora*
These include all hybrids that have, and will be, derived from crossing the above species. It was the first cross between an American and an Asiatic

'Caerhays Surprise' flowers from three years of age. It is such a marvellous magnolia it should be more easily obtainable than it is. If you spot one in a nursery buy it!

species and was made more than 40 years ago by Evamaria Sperber, who worked at the Brooklyn Botanic Garden, New York. The type clone was named 'Evamaria' and registered in 1970.

Cultivars of *M.* x *Brooklynensis* 'Evamaria'

The flowers appear after the leaves have come out in late spring and continue for a long period, often until early summer. The scentless flowers are multi-coloured, with shades of magenta rose, peach yellow and green and get darker towards the end of their flowering season. Their size is intermediate between the parents. The colour on the inside is a pale creamy-pink, dull by

comparison, but as the flowers do not open fully, this is of no consequence.

Although the plant is not very spectacular in flower because the leaves obscure them, their colouration is unique. The growth is vigorous and it will become a small to medium sized tree. It has a habit of not keeping a strong leader and therefore has a tendency to become multi-stemmed. It starts to flower from five years of age.

'Hattie Carthan'

M. x *brooklynensis*
x 'Evamaria'
The flowers do not have the pronounced purple colouration like the other two, but are yellow, green near the base, with only a slight hint of purple. Someone obviously liked it.

'Woodsman'
M. acuminata 'Klassen'
x *M. liliiflora* 'O'Neill'
Similar to 'Evamaria'
but the flowers are darker,
and the buds are very
dark purple.

'Butterflies'
M. acuminata x *M.
denudata* 'Sawada's
Cream'
This hybrid was raised in
the U.S.A. by Phil Savage.
It is reputed to have the
darkest yellow flowers
of any of the precocious
magnolia hybrids to date,
and therefore is very
sought after.

My plant is now seven
years old and 2.5m (8ft)
in height and has yet to
produce flowers.

'Caerhays Belle'
M. sargentiana
var. *robusta*
x *M. sprengeri* 'Diva'
This magnolia was bred
at Caerhays Castle in
Cornwall in 1951. It is
a vigorous tree with large,
precocious, pale pink flowers up to 27cm (11in)
wide. The individual tepals
are cupped and very broad.

'Caerhays Surprise'
M. campbellii var. *mollicomata* x *M. liliiflora* 'Nigra'
Hybridised in 1959 by
Philip Tregunna, head
gardener at Caerhays
Castle, Cornwall. I con-
sider this the finest hand-
pollinated hybrid raised in
Britain. The flowers are
20cm (8in) across and the

first six tepals open fully
into an open star-shape,
the inner six tepals open
gradually, typical of its *M.
campbellii* parent.

The flowers are produced
with great profusion and
start to open in mid-
spring, with a succession
of flower for three weeks.
The flower colour is rich
purple, which fades to
pinkish lavender as they
mature. It has a compact
habit when grown in the
open, and is fairly slow-
growing, so is ideal for the
medium sized garden.

Sadly it is not often
available from nurseries.
It is not the easiest of
plants to propagate. Not
that it does not root easily,
but it usually sets so much
flower bud it is difficult to
find suitable vegetative
growth for propagation.

'Cecil Nice'
M. denudata x *M. sargentiana* var. *robusta* ?
A seedling that grows at
Nymans in Sussex. The
flowers open in mid-spring
at the same time as the car-
pets of daffodils. The flowers are pure white, scented
and have nine tepals. It has
an attractive boss of red
stamens. In time it will
make a medium sized tree
with a fastigiate habit.
It was named after the
previous head gardener.

'Caerhays
Belle' The
original plant
at Caerhays
Castle in
Cornwall.
A beautiful
sight at the
end of the
drive wetting
the appetite
for the
botanical
treasures
that lie
beyond

'Charles Coates'
M. sieboldii x *M. tripetala*
This open-pollinated
hybrid was found growing
in the Azalea Garden at the
Royal Botanic Gardens,
Kew in 1946 by a propaga-
tor, after whom the plant
was named.

I am not too enthralled
with it as a garden plant,
and would certainly not
grow it in a prominent
position. When young it
grows rapidly and
becomes very bushy,
so commanding a lot of
space. It starts to flower in
late spring, by which time
the leaves can be up to
35cm (1¼ft) long.
The flowers are lemon
scented when young and

are pure white, 18cm (7in)
across, open out flat and
have a wrinkled surface.
The flowers have a bright
red boss of stamens in the
centre so the individual
flowers are not unattrac-
tive. However, the flowers
are very short-lived, seldom produced in abun-
dance and during sunny
and wet periods, discolour
within a day, and stay
withered on the plant for a
long time. What unblem-
ished bloom you do get is
often concealed by the
large leaves.

Tilgates, David Clulow's garden in Surrey which, before its demise, had the largest collection of magnolias in Britain.

The flowers resemble those of a small *Magnolia campbellii* var. *alba*. They open in mid-spring and are pure white, 23cm (9in) wide. It starts to flower at four years of age, and grows into a medium sized tree.

'Charles Raffill'

M. campbellii x *M. campbellii* var. *mollicomata*
This cross was made by Charles Raffill at the Royal Botanic Gardens, Kew in 1946. He had a good chance of success because the mother plant of Magnolia campbellii grew in the protected environment of the Temperate House. The intention was to create a plant that would have bright pink flowers, which would bloom later to avoid bad weather and for the flower to have a more upright poise; all this he achieved.

Approximately 100 seedlings were raised and distributed to various gardens. The Crown Estate Commissioners received several seedlings of this cross in 1949. The first of these flowered in the Valley Gardens at Windsor Great Park during mid-spring 1959 and was named 'Charles Raffill'.

The flowers open to 23cm (9in) across and are bright pink-purple, with a slight scent. It grows into a medium to large broad, spreading tree.

The seedlings raised in other gardens have also proved excellent plants. Personally I prefer that grown at Caerhays Castle named 'Kew's Surprise', which I consider has a more radiant colour.

Above: One of the original plants distributed by Kew Gardens. This plant growing in the Valley Gardens in Windsor Great Park was selected and named 'Charles Raffill'

Right: 'David Clulow' has only recently become available from specialist nurseries in Britain. It is well worth seeking out

'David Clulow'

(*M.* x *soulangeana* 'Lennei Alba') x (*M.* x *veitchii*) ?
Ken Durio of Louisiana Nursery selected this Gresham hybrid. It is considered to be one of the best white magnolias in cultivation. The original introduction to Britain was in 1985 and was grown at

'Elisa Odenwald'

(*M.* x *soulangeana* 'Lennei Alba') x *M.* x *veitchii*
This is one of the many superb hybrids raised by Todd Gresham of Santa Cruz in the U.S.A. By the time of his death in 1969 he had produced an astonishing 15,500 magnolia hybrids.

At first, I did not consider this one of great beauty, but it is slowly making an impression on me. The bowl-shaped flowers are creamy-white, fragrant, not particularly large, but they stand well poised on the bare stems in the spring, giving it a distinctive appearance. It will attain the same dimensions as its *Magnolia x soulangeana* parent.

'Elisabeth Holman'
M. campbellii var. *mollicomata* 'Lanarth'
A seedling grown at Nigel Holman's garden at Chyverton in Cornwall. It was assumed to be a hybrid with *Magnolia sargentiana* var. *robusta*, but shows no indication of this. The flowers are very similar to those of 'Lanarth'.

'Elizabeth'
M. acuminata x *M. denudata*
This was introduced to Britain in the 1980s, and was the first yellow hybrid available. The cross was carried out in 1956 by Evamaria Sperber at the Brooklyn Botanic Garden in the U.S.A.

The floral impact in Britain is variable depending on the season; some years it is totally precocious, others it flowers when the leaves are already emerging, losing

some of the effect. The flowers are pale yellow, with a very slight scent and up to 15cm (6in) across when fully open.

It has an upright habit when grown in the open and is of vigourous growth, eventually becoming a small to medium sized tree. It is very hardy, but occasionally the flowers can be damaged by late spring frosts.

Above: For the time being 'Elizabeth' is still one of the best yellow magnolias available

Below: *Magnolia* 'Elizabeth' is at its best when the flowers appear before the leaves

Many new yellow hybrids have been arriving from America during the past decade, some of which have darker flowers, but as yet no other yellow magnolia is available that equals the overall quality of this beautiful plant.

'Felix Jury'
A magnificent hybrid raised by Mark Jury in New Zealand and named after his father. It was first released in 1998. The flowers are exceptionally large, magenta in colour and produced at a very young age.

'Fireglow'
M. cylindrica x M. denudata 'Sawada's Pink'
A hybrid with an interesting parentage which I was eager to see in flower. It is hardy, has a good fastigiate growth habit and is fairly slow-growing. When it did flower I was disappointed; the flowers are small, white with a crimson base, but like many plants a definitive judgement can not be made until maturity.

'Forrest's Pink'
M. denudata x *M. sprengeri* ?
This is often listed as a cultivar of *Magnolia denudata*, but to me the colour and size of the flower is more typical of *Magnolia sprengeri*. The origins of this plant are unclear; George Forrest may have sent the seed to Caerhays Castle, and a resulting seedling was planted in 1925. Whether it was a natural hybrid or one of garden origin we will never know.

Left: 'George Henry Kern' is ideal for the small garden and gives an exceptionally long show of flowers

Opposite: 'Galaxy' is a good free-flowering magnolia. It has slightly larger and less erect flowers than its sister seedling 'Spectrum'

When I first saw the plant at Caerhays in 1981 on a dull rainy day, I was not too impressed, but having seen it in many gardens since I now rate it very highly. The flowers are large, fragrant and up to 20cm (8in) wide on a young plant. The clear pink colour on the outside of the flower is among the best of the instant bloomers, the inside of the flower is almost white. The growth is thin and vigorous and it will become a small, dense tree. Whatever its parentage, it is a most striking magnolia.

'Frank Gladney'
M. campbellii
x Gresham Hybrid ?
Almost an instant-flowering *Magnolia campbellii* but lacks the rich pink colour. The flower is pink and has the typical cup-and-saucer shape. However, it has two advantages; it flowers at least one month later, so usually escapes those fearful spring frosts and it is also very hardy. The flowers are 25cm (10in) across and creamy-white on the inside. I doubt if it will reach *Magnolia campbellii* proportions, but it will still make a large tree.

'Freeman'
M. grandiflora
x *M. virginiana*
This hybrid was raised at the U.S. National Arboretum, Washington D.C. in 1931. It has a compact, shrubby habit, which is more suitable for the smaller garden. The leaves are its main attraction, which are very dark and glossy. It flowers during mid-summer and sporadically throughout the summer, with strongly scented lemon flowers. It is the flowers that let this hybrid down; the flowers do not open fully like a *Magnolia grandiflora* or *Magnolia virginiana* , but always remain half-closed. For this reason I would grow its sister seedling, 'Maryland', or either of its parents, in preference.

'Galaxy'
M. liliiflora 'Nigra'
x *M. sprengeri* 'Diva'
This was raised at the U.S. National Arboretum in 1963. The flowers are a deep red-pink at the base fading to pale pink towards the top, and always erectly held on the naked branches.
It flowers during late spring, often escaping late frosts. It grows into a single-stemmed pyramidal tree, flowering from five years of age. Its sister seedling 'Spectrum' is very similar and perhaps preferable.

'George Henry Kern'
M. stellata x *M. liliiflora*
There are not many magnolias that are really suitable for the small garden, but this little magnolia is one of them. Admittedly you will not go into raptures over the scentless flowers, which are deep purple in bud, opening to very pale pink. What is exceptional, though, is the length of time it continues to flower, which starts in mid-spring and continues through to early summer. It is very compact, totally hardy, and will grow in full sun. The seedling was named by Carl E Kern of South Ohio in 1948 to commemorate his son, who was killed in France on V.E. Day.

'Gold Star'

M. acuminata var. *subcordata* 'Miss Honeybee'
x *M. stellata* 'Rubra'
A hybrid raised by Phil Savage of Michigan in the USA. When I first heard of a yellow *Magnolia stellata*, it sounded too good to be true. I was slightly sceptical about how yellow it would be. After seeing the plant in flower, I realised my scepticism was totally unjustified - it really is yellow and quite stunning, adding a valuable addition to the range of cultivars.

It flowers in mid-spring before the leaves come out and they are 10cm (4in) wide with 13 to 15 tepals. The leaves are larger and rounder than those of a typical *Magnolia stellata* and the new foliage has a distinct maroon-red colouration. It will start to

Left:
Magnolia 'Gold Star' is a highly desirable cultivar, which is only recently becoming available from specialist nurseries

flower from four years of age and will eventually grow into a large shrub or small tree.

'Harold Hillier'

Unknown Parentage
This magnificent magnolia arose by misfortune. A large limb of a tree fell on a grafted magnolia in Nigel Holman's garden at Chyverton in Cornwall. It was fortuitous in this case that the growth which

Below:
'Harold Hillier' is one of the best white '*M. campbellii* type' flowers

came from the rootstock was left to grow.

The very large, pure white cup-and-saucer shaped flowers, appearing in mid-spring are sensational. The rootstock that was used for the original grafted plant was raised from seed collected at Caerhays Castle, so its true parentage will never be known, but it is assumed to be a seedling of *Magnolia campbellii* var. *alba*, so is destined to become a large tree.

'Heaven Scent'

M. liliiflora x (*M.* x *veitchii*)
Considered by some to be one of the best Gresham hybrids, but this is not an opinion I agree with at all. The flowers appear in mid-spring are dull pink in colour. The name is also misleading, as the flowers do not have a heavenly scent as it suggests. It does flower very prolifically from an early age, and grows into a broadly spreading, small tree. Being very hardy it might perform better in a cold climate.

'Highdownensis'

There has been much debate and confusion regarding the classification of this plant. It has been considered a cultivar of both *Magnolia wilsonii* and *Magnolia sinensis*, and also a hybrid of the two. It was a seedling raised at Caerhays Castle and given

to Sir Frederic Stern at Highdown in Sussex.

It is thought that the flower of the *Magnolia sinensis*, which the seed came from, had been pollinated by a *Magnolia wilsonii* that was growing a few yards away. The differences of this cultivar are not pronounced, and are of no greater ornamental value of either of its assumed parents. Its main claim to fame is that it grew well on the alkaline soils at Highdown, and has been recommended as the 'best' magnolia to grow in those conditions.

'Iolanthe'

'Mark Jury'
x (*M.* x *soulangeana* 'Lennei')
Raised in New Zealand by Felix Jury and flowered for him in 1970 at four years from seed. This was the first Jury hybrid I saw in flower and what an amazing sight it was - 1.2m (4ft) high with 14 flowers. Not unusual for a magnolia, but in this case each flower was 25cm (10in) wide, a unique phenomenon. Had I been any younger I would have jumped up and down with ecstatic excitement. Now, ten years later, I have got over the initial crazed thrill and can reflect on its true merit.

It does have slight imperfections; the pale pink colour of its flowers is not as striking as it could be and the flowers are a little floppy, which is understandable considering the size and width of each tepal. The flowers also seem very frost-tender, even a slight frost as the flowers are opening will wipe out the year's bloom. It is a vigorous grower and will become a medium to large tree when it matures. When the weather is kind to it, the floral impact is remarkable. Despite its few shortcomings it is an excellent magnolia and worthy of cultivation.

'Jane'
M. stellata 'Waterlily' x *M. liliiflora* 'Reflorescens' One of the 'Little Girls' raised at the U.S. National Arboretum. It has 7.5-10cm (3-4in), slightly fragrant flowers, with 8-12 tepals, red-purple on the outside, white within. A little later flowering, starting towards the end of mid-spring, although

some years all the 'Little Girls' flower at the same time. (See also 'Ann', page 95.)

'Jersey Belle'
M. sinensis x *M. wilsonii* A hybrid raised in Jersey, Channel Islands in 1970. A beautiful plant with leaves similar to *Magnolia wilsonii* . The scented, pure white, pendulous flowers are a little larger than its parents but it is so similar it would be difficult to tell the difference without a comparative plant.

'Joe McDaniel'
M. x *soulangeana* 'Rustica Rubra' x (*M.* x *veitchii*) A Gresham hybrid which is very fastigiate and quick

growing, it has flowers that are dark violet and tulip-shaped. There is also a 'Joe McDaniel' #2, which I consider a better plant. This has flowers of the same shape and colour, but the petals fade to pure white at the top of the flower giving a good contrast. On both forms the flowers stand erect on the bare branches.

'Judy'
M. stellata x *M. liliiflora* 'Nigra' One of the 'Little Girls' from the U.S. National Arboretum. The habit is more erect than the others and is slower-growing. It has ten tepals, which are purple on the outside, white within. (See 'Ann', page 95).

Although the open flowers of *Magnolia* x *kewensis* can sometimes be damaged by frost, the plant itself is as tough as an old boot. It flowers at an early age and is of easy cultivation

M. x *kewensis*
M. kobus x *M. salicifolia* These include all hybrids that have, and will be, derived from crossing the above species. They are very hardy and of easy cultivation, growing into medium sized trees.

Cultivars of *M.* x *kewensis*
'Kew Clone'
This is the name given to the original hybrid. It was an open-pollinated seedling that was found near a *Magnolia kobus* in the Royal Botanic Gardens, Kew in 1938. It has pure white, scented flowers, which are similar to its *Magnolia kobus* parent, and open in mid-spring.

'Wada's Memory'
If the merits of a magnolia were based on the judgement of just one isolated flower this cultivar would rank almost bottom. The flowers appear in mid-spring and are fragrant and large, but look as if they are either suffering from severe heat exhaustion, dehydration or both. Its saving grace is that the flowers are produced with such abundance that *en masse* the show is extremely effective from a distance.

It is a fast-growing tree with a pyramidal habit. It was raised from seed sent to the University of Washington Arboretum, Seattle, from Koichiro Wada, a nurseryman in Japan.

The *Magnolia* x *loebneri* cultivars have many attributes: they are very hardy, of easy cultivation, tolerant of slightly alkaline soils, of moderate size and flower from an early age.

With the various cultivars ranging in size from large shrubs to medium sized trees, they contend as the most accommodating magnolias for small to medium sized gardens.

The taxonomy and nomenclature regarding this group of plants is very confusing, (See Nomenclature, page 14). At present it encompasses all the intermediate forms between *Magnolia stellata* and *Magnolia kobus*, including both intentional crosses and spontaneous hybrids, some of which I suspect may not be hybrids at all. This means there is enormous variation within the group, as both the flowers and the stature can closely resemble either parent.

'Kew's Surprise'

M. campbellii x *M. campbellii* var. *mollicomata*
This cross was made by Charles Raffill at the Royal Botanic Gardens, Kew in 1946. Two seedlings of it were sent to Caerhays Castle in Cornwall around 1951. 'Kew's Surprise' first flowered in 1966. Grafted plants start to flower from ten years of age. Surrounding trees have drawn up the original plant to a height of 15m (50ft) at Caerhays, but the mid-pink 25cm (10in) flowers look radiant against a clear blue sky. It has not been propagated as much as 'Charles Raffill' which is a pity, as I consider it a superior plant.

'Lotus'

'Mark Jury' x (*M.* x *soulangeana* 'Lennei Alba')
A New Zealand hybrid raised by Felix Jury. The flowers are 25cm (10in) wide creamy-white with spatula-shaped tepals, and attractive red stamens. It starts to flower sporadically at approximately five years of age, but does not flower with abundance until a few years later. It will develop into a medium sized tree.

Some of the leaves of *Magnolia* x *loebneri*, particularly 'Leonard Messel', can have attractive autumn colouring

Opposite: *Magnolia* x *loebneri* 'Leonard Messel' is still one of the best magnolias for general planting. It is tolerant of a wide range of soils, very hardy and always produces a mass of flowers

M. x *loebneri*

M. kobus x *M. stellata*
Magnolia x *loebneri* is the name given to all plants with *Magnolia kobus* as one parent and *Magnolia stellata* (or any of their respective cultivars) as its other parent. Max Löbner who was Garden Inspector at Dresden Botanical Gardens, made the first cross between these two species. It flowered in 1917 and in appearance was intermediate between the two parents. It grows into a small slender branched tree. The flowers are fragrant with 12 pure white tepals and appear before the leaves in mid-spring.

Cultivars of *M.* x *loebneri*

'Ballerina'

M. x loebneri 'Spring Snow' x M. stellata 'Waterlily'

It has pleasantly scented, pale pink flowers with up to 30 tepals, which turn white with age. It is slightly later-flowering than other *Magnolia* x *loebneri* cultivars and has a compact habit, making it ideal for the small garden.

'Donna'

It was selected by Harry Heineman of Scituate, Massachusetts. The 13cm (5¼in) flowers are the largest of any *Magnolia* x *loebneri* cultivar. They are fragrant, pure white and appear throughout mid-spring. It has a compact habit, and grows as wide as it does high. It was

left: The flowers of *Magnolia* x *loebneri* 'Pirouette' are pretty from the moment they open

Right: The open flower of *Magnolia* x *loebneri* 'Pirouette'

Below: *Magnolia* x *loebneri* 'Merrill' is an outstanding cultivar. This fine specimen is growing at Eisenhut's Nursery in Switzerland

introduced to Britain around 1990 and although plants are still young, it shows great potential.

'Encore'

I have not seen a large plant of this cultivar in Britain, but when I saw a 3m (12ft) plant in Switzerland I was very impressed; it was a solid mass of flower. It forms

groups of buds at the ends of the branches and on the short spurs along the branches. The flowers are white with a faint pink blush at the base and continue to come out over a long period, hence its name. It is slow-growing and has a very compact habit.

'Leonard Messel'

This is by far the most widely grown *M* x *loebneri* cultivar. It was an open-pollinated seedling of *Magnolia stellata* 'Rosea' that was assumed to have been pollinated by a nearby Magnolia kobus, and was planted at Nymans in Sussex around 1940. The flowers are pink on the outside, white within, and 10-13cm (4-5in) wide, appearing from early to mid-spring. It will eventually become a small tree up to 10m (30ft) in height. Despite its antiq-

uity it remains one of the best *M* x *loebneri* for general planting.

'Merrill'

An early *Magnolia* x *loebneri* hybrid from the Arnold Arboretum in America. When grown in the open it has a compact, broad, spreading habit, often becoming as wide as it is high. It flowers in mid spring and is a cloud of semi-double, pure white, fragrant flowers. An excellent cultivar.

'Neil McEacharn'

This was raised at Windsor Great Park from seed of *Magnolia kobus* var. *stellata* 'Rosea' growing in the gardens of Villa Taranto, Italy. The buds are very pale pink, but when open the flowers are pure white with 10-12 tepals. It will grow into a small, medium sized tree. A good cultivar in its time but has now been superseded.

'Pirouette'

A magnolia selected in Japan. A flower of a very distinctive form. The outer tepals are shorter than the central ones, giving the small, pure white flower a very pretty globular

shape, which have a delicate fragrance. This cultivar seems to be slow-growing and very shy to flower when young, only now flowering with profusion after nine years. The individual flowers are so exquisite that I always cut a few to put in a small vase.

'Powder Puff'

The flowers are slightly smaller but similar in appearance to 'Pirouette' in having the central tepals longer than the outer ones, which is most noticeable when the flower starts to open. It has a very compact, rounded habit. Although it does not produce a mass of colour, the individual flowers are very attractive.

'Raspberry Fun'

An open-pollinated seedling of 'Leonard Messel'. It is very similar to its parent but the flowers are formed in clusters. Plants in Britain are still too young to determine if it is of greater merit than its parent.

'Spring Snow'

An American selection that probably originated from open-pollinated *Magnolia stellata* seed. The flowers are pure white and fragrant, with 15-20 tepals. Young flowers have a slight green shading at the centre. It will grow into a small round-headed tree up to 8m (20ft).

'Manchu Fan'

(*M.* x *soulangeana* 'Lennei Alba') x *M.* x *veitchii*
A Gresham hybrid which in flower resembles *Magnolia denudata*, except that the flowers are larger, thicker textured and have a purple stain at the base on the outside of the tepals. It has a moderate growth, slightly more vigorous than the well-known *Magnolia* x *soulangeana*. The fragrant flowers, which open in mid-spring, are not particularly large, but are well formed, elegant, of a radiant colour and are produced at a young age in abundance. A good all-rounder for the medium sized garden.

Below: The flowers of 'Manchu Fan' are not big and blousey, but have a very refined quality to them

'Marj Gossler'

M. denudata x *M. sargentiana* var. *robusta*
An American hybrid named in 1989. The flowers appear in mid-spring and are light pink at the base on the outside, pure white within, up to 25cm (10in) wide and very fragrant. It makes vigorous growth and will become a medium sized tree. It flowers from four years of age, but they are not produced in great quantity until its initial growth has slowed down.

'Mark Jury'

M. campbellii var. *mollicomata* 'Lanarth' x *M. sargentiana* var. *robusta* ?
There could not have been a more important and useful cultivar raised this century. One would have expected this plant to have materialised after years of breeding work, but this was certainly not the case. A grafted plant of *Magnolia campbellii* var. *mollicomata* 'Lanarth' was sent by Hilliers Nursery to Felix Jury in New Zealand in about 1956 and it failed to survive, as no other grafted plants were available a

'Maryland'

M. grandiflora x
M. virginiana
The leaves are very similar to *M. grandiflora*, as are the fragrant flowers but a little smaller. It was initially selected because of its ease of propagation from cuttings. Although I rate it higher than its sister seedling, 'Freeman', I still prefer either of their parents.

'Michael Rosse'

M. campbellii var. *alba* x *M. sargentiana* var. *robusta*?
This was raised from open-pollinated seed collected from a *Magnolia campbellii* var. *alba* at Caerhays Castle. The original plant grows in the garden at Nymans in Sussex and is now a broad, spreading tree 15m (50ft) in height. The flowers appear in mid-spring and are 23cm (9in) wide, pale pink in colour, similar in shape to *M. campbellii*. 'Princess Margaret' is a possible sister seedling grown in the Valley Gardens in Windsor Great Park, and has a richer, darker pink flower and is slightly superior.

seedling from the tree at Lanarth was sent to replace it. Unlike its assumed parents, the seedling flowered at nine years of age with huge cup-and-saucer shaped, creamy-white flowers 25cm (10in) across.

I first saw 'Mark Jury' flower in April 1990 when our plant was five years old. I anticipated something extraordinary was going to happen when the hairy, ovoid flower bud grew to the size of a goose egg. I was not disappointed, I had never seen such a large flower on such a young plant.

Its importance as a magnolia is not so much for its own beauty, but for all its subsequent hybrids that have, and will be, raised using its genes. It was fortuitous that this seedling ended up with someone who was so admirably capable of utilising it to its full potential, as has been demonstrated with cultivars such as 'Atlas', 'Athene', 'Milky Way' and 'Iolanthe'.

Opposite: 'Milky Way' is another class act from New Zealand. The beauty of the arrangement and formation of the sexual parts on some of the larger flowers is often overlooked

Right: 'Mark Jury' has been one of the parents of many recently introduced hybrids from New Zealand

'Milky Way'

'Mark Jury' x
(*M.* x *soulangeana* 'Lennei Alba')
A hybrid raised in New Zealand by Felix Jury and a sister seedling of 'Athene'. The heavy-textured, fragrant flowers appear in April and are pure white with a pink blush at the base. It flowers at a young age and with greater abundance than 'Athene', but the flowers are slightly smaller. A magnificent magnolia for a medium sized garden.

'Nimbus'

M. hypoleuca
x *M. virginiana*
This cross was made at the United States National Arboretum in 1956. It is partially evergreen, retaining most of its leaves, which can be a slight disadvantage because by the end of the winter they can look decidedly tatty. When the new fresh-green leaves have grown by late spring the foliage is very attractive, with leaves up to 36cm (14in) long. The creamy-white flowers are 15cm (6in) wide and produced from three years of

age. They start to open in late spring and continue through until mid-summer.

The lemon-rose scent of the flowers is one of the strongest of any magnolia. Even while still in bud the fragrance is remarkably powerful. Once established it grows very vigorously, occasionally producing shoots 1m (3ft) long. Because of its amazing scent, and the attractive flowers and foliage, it is a magnolia to be highly recommended.

Unfortunately, it is notoriously difficult to root from cuttings. The greatest success is by propagating it early in the season using softwood cuttings. For this reason it will never be available in large quantities and those plants which are sold are usually grafted.

'Orchid'

M. liliiflora x *M. stellata*
There are some orchids I do not consider beautiful and this magnolia likewise. It has a compact, shrubby habit. The flowers are produced during mid- to late Spring and are dark red-purple, small, scentless and do not open fully. In her book on magnolias, Dorothy Callaway states that 'The principle virtue of this hybrid is that it is hardier than either parent' I consider this its only virtue!

'Paul Cook'

(*M.* x *soulangeana* 'Lennei' seedling) x *M. sprengeri* 'Diva'
This magnolia was raised in America and demonstrates well what is meant by the term 'hybrid vigour'. It grows more rapidly than any other magnolia I know. When young the terminal growth can put on 1m (3ft) a year. This growth is not to its advantage; the plant becomes very weak and gaunt.

Plants start to flower at four years of age, by which time it may be 3.5m (11ft) high. The fragrant flowers open in mid- spring, are 25cm (10in) wide, and have very broad overlapping tepals. The flowers hang on the branches in all directions, giving you the opportunity to see the pure white insides of the large flower. Because of its habit, its long-term ornamental use is debatable, but time will tell.

Above left:
If you appreciate scent in the garden you would not be disappointed with the powerful lemon-rose fragrance of 'Nimbus'

Below:
'Philip Tregunna' is one of the most stunningly beautiful magnolias grown in the gardens at Caerhays Castle in Cornwall

'Peppermint Stick'

M. liliiflora x (*M.* x *veitchii*)
This is a Gresham Hybrid and named by the breeders in 1962. The flowers appear on naked branches in mid- spring and are white with purple marking sat the base and the centre of the tepals. They sit on the branches with a neat, erect poise, and never open flat. The plant itself is distinguishable by its compact, fastigiate habit, making it useful for confined areas.

'Peter Smithers'

(*M.* x *soulangeana* 'Rustica Rubra') x (*M.* x *veitchii*)
A Gresham hybrid which was named in 1985 in honour of the great plantsman, Sir Peter Smithers of Ticino, Switzerland.

Not a particularly attractive colour when the flower first opens, but it has a good shape and colour when mature. The flowers open in mid-spring and are pink-purple on the outside, almost white within and up to 20cm (8in) across.

'Philip Tregunna'

M. campbellii x *M. sargentiana* var. *robusta*
A hybrid raised at Caerhays Castle, Cornwall in 1960 and named in honour of the long- serving and highly regarded Head Gardener who started working at Caerhays in 1944.

Apart from the many large Asiatic magnolia species grown at Caerhays, there are also numerous seedlings. After spending a day studying the hundreds of magnolias there, it was an unnamed seedling that I considered one of the most stunning. The glowing purplish colour of the large flowers is quite exceptional. It is a very robust grower, eventually making a large tree.

It does not flower as a young plant; a wait of at least ten years is necessary, but with its healthy, dark green foliage and vigorous growth it is a pleasure to watch it grow in the interim period. It was officially named on 10 March 1992 when it was awarded a First Class Certificate by the Royal Horticultural Society.

Pickard's Selections

M. x soulangeana x 'Picture Seedling' x ?
Amos Pickard of Canterbury in Kent lined out 120 open-pollinated seedlings, taken from a seedling of *Magnolia x soulangeana* 'Picture', which had pure white flowers. Of the 120 seedlings 15 were selected as being superior and were first offered for sale in 1974.

All are vigorous plants with upright growth; the flowers are fragrant and are mainly large with broad tepals and goblet-shaped, except *Magnolia* 'Pickard's Schmetterling'. They are hardy and flower before the leaves in mid- to late spring.

While some are still worthy of cultivation, particularly 'Garnet', 'Ruby' and 'Schmetterling', many have been surpassed by more recent Gresham and Jury hybrids. The description of colours is based on plants grown in Britain. Pickard's cultivars grown in Switzerland have an amazingly deep intensity to the colour, to the extent that they are incomparable to plants grown in England. Thinking that we grew incorrectly named plants, propagation material was taken from the Swiss plants and grown alongside the same cultivars in Britain, but the flower colour was identical. This phenomenon may be caused by the difference in the spectrum of light, temperature or nutrient content of the soil, or a combination of all three.

Of all the Pickard's hybrids that were raised 'Pickard's Schmetterling' is one of the best-coloured cultivars among them

The Pickard cultivars listed below were registered in 1984.

'Pickard's Charm' Pink flowers that are slightly tulip-shaped.

'Pickard's Coral' Flowers white with a very faint pink flush.

'Pickard's Cornelian' Flowers pure white at the top shading to a deep wine-red at the base.

'Pickard's Crystal' Flowers similar to 'Coral' but a deeper pink flush.

'Pickard's Firefly' Flowers large with deep wine-red colouration at base.

'Pickard's Garnet' Large, deep wine-red flowers with white shading at top of tepal.

'Pickard's Glow' Similar to above but slightly smaller flowers.

'Pickard's Maime' Large flowers, wine-red at base and a line going up the middle of tepal.

'Pickard's Opal' Pure white flowers with faint rose flush at base.

'Pickard's Pearl' Small flowers similar to above.

'Pickard's Pink Diamond' Flowers large, pure white with faint pink flush at base.

'Pickard's Ruby' Flowers almost entirely wine-red to purple.

'Pickard's Schmetterling' Long, deep wine-red tepals on the outside, almost white within.

'Pickard's Snow Queen' Very large, pure white flowers.

'Pickard's Stardust'
M. kobus x ?
This is a hybrid of *Magnolia kobus* of uncertain origin. A compact plant that will grow into a small tree. The pure white, fragrant flowers have up to 12 tepals and look very similar to a *Magnolia* x *loebneri* hybrid. Because of its floriferous nature from a young age, it is a commendable garden plant.

'Pinkie'
M. stellata 'Rosea' x *M. liliiflora* 'Reflorescens'
One of the eight 'Little Girl' hybrids from the U.S. National Arboretum, I think this variety is the most worthy. It has the most distinct flowers of the group, which are cup-shaped, 13cm (5in) wide, pale pink on the outside, white within and appear from mid-spring. (See 'Ann', page 95.)

'Princess Margaret'
M. campbellii var. *alba* x *M. sargentiana* var. *robusta* ?
This was raised from open-pollinated seed collected from a *Magnolia campbellii* var. *alba* at Caerhays Castle; the male parent could have been one of the several species in the vicinity. Some of these seedlings were sent to Windsor Great Park and nine of them were planted in a group in the Valley Gardens in 1960. When they flowered, one stood out amongst all the others, it was not the largest flowered, but the colour was an exceptional rich pink.

It is a vigorous plant, growing into a large tree. The flowers are up to 25cm (10in) wide and appear during mid-spring. 'Michael Rosse' is a sister seedling growing at Nymans in Sussex.

'Pristine'
M. denudata x *M. stellata* 'Waterlily'
A lovely introduction from America. The flowers are pure white, similar to those of *Magnolia denudata*, but with double the number of tepals and flowering slightly later. A grafted plant will flower from four years of age and will grow into a very hardy small tree.

M. x *proctoriana*
M. salicifolia x *M. stellata*
These include all hybrids that have, and will be, derived from crossing the above species. The type clone was an open-pollinated seedling found in an arboretum owned by a T E Proctor of Massachusetts, and was selected by the Arnold Arboretum in 1928.

The flowers are relatively small, pure white, fragrant and have six or more tepals. They open in mid-spring and are often slightly curved. It grows into a small tree with very slender branches. Generally not considered a tree of exceptional beauty.

'Purple Eye'
M. denudata x ?
It is a shame that this beautiful cultivar is not grown more often. It was a seedling that was given to Peter Veitch, the famous nurseryman from J C Williams of Caerhays Castle. Its parentage is unknown but it is presumed to be a hybrid with *Magnolia* x *soulangeana*. The fragrant flowers are large, bowl-shaped, pure white with purple staining at the base and appear during mid-spring on leafless branches. It has a broad, spreading growth habit, typical of *Magnolia denudata*.

'Purple Globe'
M. liliiflora 'Nigra' x (*M.* x *veitchii*)
Raised by Oswald Blumhardt in New Zealand and introduced to Britain in 1989. The flowers are a radiant pink-purple, paler within and 20cm (8in) wide. Like his other hybrid, *Magnolia* 'Star Wars', it has an exceptionally long flowering period which starts in mid-spring and continues until early summer. It is a vigourous plant, with an open habit. Often incorrectly named as 'Purple Glow'.

Left:
A young plant of 'Princess Margaret' growing within the rhododendron species collection in Windsor Great Park

'Purple Prince'

M. liliiflora 'Darkest Purple' x (*M. x soulangeana* 'Lennei') Introduced to Britain in 1989 from America. The exceptionally dark flowers are 20cm (8in) wide with six tepals, which are a vivid dark purple on the outside, slightly paler within. It will eventually grow into a large shrub or small tree.

'Randy'

M. liliiflora 'Nigra' x *M. stellata* One of the eight 'Little Girl' hybrids from the U.S. National Arboretum, and another one that does not do much for me. The flowers have eight to eleven narrow tepals, which are dark pink on the outside, white within. (See 'Ann', page 95.)

'Ricki'

M. liliiflora 'Nigra' x *M. stellata* Another of the 'Little Girl' hybrids from the U.S. National Arboretum. The flowers are 15cm (6in) wide, the 10-15 tepals are often twisted. Not very inspiring. (See 'Ann', page 95.)

'Rouged Alabaster'

(*M. x soulangeana* 'Lennei Alba') x (*M. x veitchii*) The flowers open in early spring and are large, bowl-shaped, very fragrant and pure white with a pink blush at the base. They are very thick-textured and measure 25cm (10in) across. It flowers from a young age, and will rapidly grow into a small tree.

'Purple Globe' is not as well known as it should be, few people grow this good-looking newcomer from New Zealand

'Royal Crown'

M. liliiflora x (*M. x veitchii*) A Gresham Hybrid with 25cm (10in) dark red to violet flowers with 12 tepals that are white within. It was named by Todd Gresham in 1962. There are plants grown in Britain that have white flowers with red veining which are incorrectly named as this cultivar.

'Sayonara'

M. liliiflora x (*M. x veitchii*) A Gresham hybrid raised in America in 1955 and introduced to Britain by Sir Harold Hillier in 1963. The scented flowers are globular in shape, creamy-white, with a dark pink-purple flush at the base. The flower has up to 12 tepals and when fully open measures 20cm (8in) across. It forms a small, broad-headed tree and flowers at a young age.

'Serene'

M. liliiflora x 'Mark Jury' A New Zealand hybrid raised by Felix Jury. The flowers are large and dark pink, white on the inside. As the flower opens the outer tepals lie horizon-tally, leaving the inner tepals cupped; the contrast of the two colours is very attractive. The flowers start opening in mid-spring and are very dark, it is a slight anticlimax that the flowers do not stay that colour, but fade to a mid-pink. It is moderately vigorous and will become a small to medium sized tree.

'Spectrum'

M. liliiflora 'Nigra' x *M. sprengeri* 'Diva' A hybrid made at the U.S. National Arboretum in 1963. It flowers in mid-spring, just before the leaves appear and, hope-fully, after any severe late frosts. The flowers are deep reddish-pink on the out-side, creamy-white within and have an erect poise; the ends of the tepals usu-ally reflex outwards. It grows vigorously and will become a broad-headed, medium sized tree. It is very similar to its sister seedling 'Galaxy', but the flowers of 'Spectrum' are slightly darker. It flow-ers from six years of age.

M. x soulangeana

M. denudata x *M. liliiflora* This hybrid was made in France by Etienne Soulange-Bodin in 1820. It is the most widely grown magnolia, not only in Britain, but world-wide. It is of easy cultivation tolerating wind, a wide variety of soil types and is very hardy. Its eventual size is often underesti-mated, as many suburban garden owners know only too well. When given enough space they grow into large, broad-spread-ing, multi-stemmed shrubs, eventually attain-ing a tree-like stature.

Left: Despite having been around for many years some *Magnolia x soulangeana* hybrids such as 'Alexandrina' still hold their own when it comes to producing a spectacular display

There are now over 40 *Magnolia x soulangeana* cultivars, many of which, like the original, were raised during the last century. The colour of the flower ranges from pure white through to dark purple, many are so similar that it is difficult to distinguish them from each other. They all have a slight fragrance, which can only be appreciated when in close proximity. Their main flowering period is during mid-spring before the leaves appear, and occasionally they have a light flowering during late summer.

Cultivars

Outlined below are some of the most worthy and distinct cultivars of *Magnolia x soulangeana*

'Alba Superba'

Elegant, candle-shaped buds that open into pure white flowers; very often white-flowered seedlings are grown under this name.

'Alexandrina'

The flowers are cerise-pink at the base fading through to pure white near the top. One of the best-coloured and most floriferous cultivars.

'Amabilis'

Buds are white and have a yellowish colouration at the base; mature flowers are pure white developing the faintest flush of pink at the base.

'Brozzonii'

Often referred to as the aristocrat among the *Magnolia x soulangeana* cultivars. The flowers are white with a slight pink flush near the base, and have a graceful poise on the sweeping branches. A great asset is that it flowers two weeks later than the others do, so often escaping spring frosts.

'Etienne Soulange-Bodin'

The name often given to what is considered to be the original hybrid, and is usually the plant frequently seen and sold as Magnolia x soulangeana

'Lennei'

This has large, bowl-shaped flowers. It has the darkest flowers of all the *Magnolia x soulangeana* cultivars, which are deep vinous-purple on the outside and white within. Unfortunately, it is a most untidy grower with long straggly branches that cross in every direction.

'Lennei Alba'

Very large, ivory-white, goblet-shaped flowers. It has been used extensively as the seed parent for hybridising. It is similar to

Below: Although 'Picture' is considered a *Magnolia x soulangeana* hybrid it is distinct from all the others

Magnolia denudata, but the flowers are larger, not such a pure white and the three outer tepals are smaller than the inner tepals. One of the best white cultivars.

'Picture'

It was discovered in Japan in about 1930, its parentage is uncertain, as it is so different from any other Magnolia x soulangeana cultivar. It has by far the largest flowers, measuring up to 27cm (11in) across when fully open, not globular, but more cup-and-saucer-shaped. The flowers are dark purple at the base fading to pink, edged with white on the outside and white within.

'Rustica Rubra'

A commonly grown cultivar of Dutch origin, and is assumed to be a seedling of *Magnolia x soulangeana* 'Lennei', which it most closely resembles. The flowers have a strong fragrance, are goblet-shaped, pale maroon on the outside, milky white within.

'San José'

An American introduction which originated in 1938. Unfortunately, most of the plants grown in Britain, including the plant given an Award of Merit by the Royal Horticultural Society in 1987, are different from the original plants grown in America. The flowers here are white with a dark pink flush at the base of the flower, a pink line extends up the middle of the tepal. These are produced in abundance on a densely branched, compact plant. The original plant in America has very large, dark flowers that are similar to 'Lennei'.

'Star Wars'

M. campbellii x *M. liliiflora*
For me to choose my top ten magnolias would be very difficult, but *Magnolia* 'Star Wars' would certainly be one of them. It is a near-perfect magnolia for a large garden. It was raised in New Zealand by Oswald Blumhardt during the 1970s, and was introduced to Britain in 1985.

The flowers are bright pink on the outside, almost white within and measure 27cm (11in) wide. It has an exceptionally long flowering season, starting in mid-spring, with flowers appearing until late spring. The flowers are produced prolifically on plants from four years of age, at five years my plant had 70 flowers which, bearing in mind the size of each flower, was quite remarkable. The plant will grow into a large, symmetrical-shaped tree.

It is also a propagator's dream since, like its *Magnolia liliiflora* parent, cuttings root with ease, so it is destined for a great future. The one and only fault this plant has is that the flowers are devoid of any scent but, taking into account its floral impact and overall beauty, this really is a minor imperfection.

'Susan'

M. stellata 'Rosea'
x *M. liliiflora* 'Nigra'
One of the eight 'Little Girl' hybrids from the U.S. National Arboretum. The slightly fragrant flowers are dark purple inside and out and have six tepals, which can be twisted. It starts flowering in mid-spring and continues for four weeks. Do not buy one to give to a Susan; she might not be too flattered! (See 'Ann', page 95.)

'Sweet Sixteen'

(*M.* x *soulangeana* 'Lennei Alba') x (*M.* x *veitchii*)
A Gresham hybrid introduced to Britain around 1986. It has long, tapered, candle-like buds, which open in mid-spring into pristine white, tulip-shaped flowers, eventually becoming cup-shaped and 20cm (8in) wide. A vigorous grower, becoming a round, oval tree.

Above:
The amount of flower this true form of *Magnolia* x *soulangeana* 'San Jose' produces is almost unequalled in the genus

Below: The radiant pink flowers of 'Star Wars' and the beautiful white flowers of *Magnolia* x *loebneri* 'Encore'

M. x *thompsoniana*

M. tripetala x *M. virginiana*
These include all hybrids that have, and will be, derived from crossing the above species. This is the first known magnolia hybrid to be raised in the western world. It was grown from seed that was assumed to have been pollinated by a nearby *Magnolia tripetala* in Archibald Thompson's nursery at Mile End, London in 1808.

If this was the case, it was a lucky cross because, although *Magnolia virginiana* occasionally produces seed in Britain, I have not managed to germinate it, suggesting it is usually infertile. It is more probable that fertile seed was sent from America.

Cultivars of *M.* x *thompsoniana* 'Thompsoniana'

This is the type clone. Although not spectacular, it starts to flower at a young age, with flowers that are creamy-yellow and remaining vase-shaped for a long time. They have a pleasant fragrance, similar to its *Magnolia virginiana* parent. It has a long flowering period, which starts in late spring and continues sporadically until mid summer. The growth is very untidy with branches twisting and bending in all directions so it will grow into a large shrub, rather than a small tree. The leaves can be up to 25cm (10in) long and are glossy green above, silvery underneath. It is almost evergreen, losing the leaves towards the end of the winter.

'Urbana'

A cross made in 1960 in America. It is very similar to the type clone.

'Tiffany'
(*M.* x *veitchii*) x ?
A Gresham hybrid with very large, fragrant flowers which are white with a pronounced pink base. They are so large and heavily textured that when they open in mid-spring the flowers often flop over sideways as the twigs can not support them. Like most of the Gresham hybrids it is a very vigorous grower.

'Tina Durio'
(M. x *soulangeana* 'Lennei Alba') x (*M.* x *veitchii*)
One of the best Gresham hybrids. The fragrant, heavy-textured flowers

open in mid-spring and are pure white, with the faintest pink blush at the base, measuring up to 25cm (10in) wide. It is a vigorously growing plant, becoming a medium sized tree. Very desirable!

M. x *veitchii*
M. *campbellii* x
M. *denudata*
These include all hybrids that have, and will be, derived from crossing the above species. This hybrid was raised by Peter Veitch, a nurseryman in Exeter, in 1907 and is possibly the first hand-pollinated cross of a magnolia in Britain.

Magnolia x *veitchii* 'Peter Veitch' growing in the Savill Gardens in Windsor Great Park. Compared to the dimensions of some, this one is still a juvenile

Cultivars of *M.* x *veitichii*
'Peter Veitch'
It is the tallest-growing magnolia which, given favourable conditions, can reach 30m (100ft) in height. Its potential size restricts its use, so it is only suitable for very large gardens. It has a great advantage in that it flowers at the same time as the leaves come out at the end of spring. This is usually late enough to escape the spring frosts, and is useful for extending the magnolia flowering season. Being one of the last precocious magnolias to flower it is easily recognised. The light pink opening buds are candle-like, and are produced in great abundance. On mature trees with the flowers fully open, the effect is like a white cloud in the sky.

Because of its rapid growth the branches are very prone to wind damage, so a sheltered sight is always necessary. It has inherited the *Magnolia campbellii* trait of not flowering as a young plant; a ten-year wait is not unusual.

'Isca'
This was selected from the same batch of seedlings as the previous cultivar. The growth is slower and the flowers are pale pink in bud, opening to almost pure white. It is named after a town near Exeter.

'Vulcan'
M. campbellii var. *mollicomata* 'Lanarth' x *M. liliiflora* hybrid
A hybrid raised in New Zealand by Felix Jury and introduced to Britain in 1989. It was thought by those who saw the original plant in New Zealand to be the ultimate hybrid. The colour of the flower was considered unique, and a true colour break, being brilliant ruby-red. It flowers from three years of age, but the flowers are at first a dirty purple, very small and quite insignificant.

Now, ten years after it was introduced, the plant has still not produced flowers that are comparable in size or colour to its New Zealand parent. However, the flowers are a dark radiant pink, and have increased to 23cm (9in) in width. If the metamorphosis to transform this plant never takes place in Britain, it is still worth growing. I feel optimistic that this plant will improve with age.

'Wada's Snow White'

M. denudata x
M. salicifolia
This bi-specific hybrid was raised by K Wada in Japan and introduced by Sir Peter Smithers. The white, fragrant flowers have eight to nine tepals and always stand erect on the slender branches. It flowers in mid-spring and from a young age. It has a slow spreading habit.

M. x *wieseneri*

M. hypoleuca
x *M. sieboldii*
A genuine antique from the Orient, and a great treasure to have in the garden. This magnolia probably arose as an open-pollinated hybrid in Japan, where the two parents are natives. It was introduced into Britain when a plant was purchased from the International Paris Expo in 1889 by the Royal Botanic Gardens, Kew.

The 15cm (6in) flowers are of exceptional beauty, the prominent red and pink stamens contrast brilliantly with the creamy-white tepals of the upward-facing flowers. They start to open at the beginning of early summer

Right: The flowers of *Magnolia* x *wieseneri* are one of the most attractive of the genus

Below: Despite possibly being the first 'Vulcan' in Britain it still bears immature flowers, but they do seem to get bigger each year

and continue sporadically through to mid-summer. The pleasant fragrance emitted by the flowers is particularly strong and is usually smelt before the flower is seen.

Its growth habit is variable, some mature specimens are squat, with intermingled branches, others grow into respectably shaped, small trees. It is probable that more than one clone is cultivated, and the growth habit may be one of the differentiating features. It starts to flower from three years of age.

'Yellow Bird'

M. acuminata x (*M.* x *brooklynensis* 'Evamaria')
Introduced to Britain in 1986 from Brooklyn Botanic Garden, New York. The bright yellow flowers are tulip-shaped and usually remain so until the tepals fall off, therefore they seldom open fully. They come out at the same

time as the leaves in late spring and continue for three weeks. The first flowers are very noticeable and make an impressive display, but the fresh green leaves conceal subsequent flowers.

It has a very vigorous and fastigiate habit and commences flowering from five years of age. The flowers look effective when cut and placed in a vase, as they then open out fully. The impact of a large tree in flower in Britain cannot as yet be assessed, but not being particularly precocious, it might not be that spectacular.

Plants in the Same Family

Other plants in the Magnoliaceae family that can be grown in Britain are *Liriodendron, Manglietia* and also *Michelia*.

Liriodendron

This genus has two species, both represented in the same distinct geographic regions as the magnolias. They are of easy cultivation, quick-growing and are tolerant of both acid and alkaline soils. The wood is quite brittle so branches can be damaged by strong, gusty winds. This usually occurs during their adolescent years; mature specimens do not suffer as much, which is just as well as they can grow into enormous trees.

Liriodendron tulipifera
Tulip Tree

This tree has been grown in Britain for around 350 years. It is a native of eastern North America, where it grows to a height of almost 60m (200ft).In Britain, it becomes a stately tree up to 30m (100ft) in height.

Its main ornamental feature is its distinctive leaves which are unlike any other tree, apart from its Chinese counterpart. The tree is at its most beautiful during the autumn when the leaves turn rich yellow.

Liriodendron chinensis is the lesser known of the two species. The flowers are greener and less conspicuous

The inconspicuous flowers are tulip-shaped, green with orange markings and appear in early to mid-summer. There are several cultivars of this species, many of which have a golden variegation on the leaf.

Liriodendron chinensis

It was introduced from China by Ernest Wilson in 1901. It is very similar to *Liriodendron tulipifera*, but smaller in all parts and the flowers are green and even less conspicuous. It does not appear to make such a large tree.

Manglietia

There are around 29 species, coming mainly from tropical areas of Asia. A few come from the more temperate regions of China, but only *Manglietia insignis* is considered hardy enough for outdoor cultivation and this has to be restricted to the warmer parts of the country.

Manglietia insignis

Native to S E Asia. It grows into a small, evergreen tree with beautiful foliage. The leaves are very glossy, dark green on the upper surface, often glaucous beneath and up to 25cm (10in)

long. The scented flowers appear in late spring on the ends of the branches and are purple when young, opening to creamy-white. Their hardiness is variable and is dependent upon where the plants were obtained in the wild. Plants in Surrey have survived temperatures of -10°C (14°F) in sheltered woodland with no die-back.

Michelia

A genus of approximately 45-50 species of evergreen trees and shrubs mainly native to tropical areas of S E Asia. They differ from magnolias because the flowers are borne along the stems at the leaf axils, often in clusters; also there is a long stalk between the gynoecium (the female part of the flower) and the androecium (the male part of the flower).

Michelia doltsopa is the only species that is relatively hardy and it is of great floral beauty. The other species are best planted in a conservatory or greenhouse where the fragrance can be appreciated.

There are hybrids now being bred in America and New Zealand which, when introduced, could soon outclass the limited varieties that we now grow. In 1988 an American bi-generic hybrid was introduced to Britain, a cross between *Magnolia acuminata* 'Miss Honeybee' and *Michelia figo*, which has proved to be totally hardy. The ability to cross-pollinate the hardy with the more tender members of the family is exciting for the future.

Michelia doltsopa

To see a large specimen in flower in one of the Cornish gardens is a great spectacle for the eyes and a heavenly treat for the nose. It starts to flower in mid-spring and has a succession of flowers for up to a month. The flowers are creamy-white, 10cm (4in) across and are powerfully fragrant. The evergreen leaves are thick and leathery and are up to 18cm (7in) long.

Both the leaf buds and the flower buds are covered in thick, copper-coloured, velvety hairs, which give you a clue that something grand is to follow. It is possible to grow this desirable plant outside in the warmer parts of Britain.

The sumptuous flowers of *Michelia doltsopa* 'Silver Cloud' and its strong evocative fragrance make it a must for anyone living in a favourable climate or for the very large conservatory

Bibliography
and Index

Bibliography

BEAN, W.J., *Trees and Shrubs Hardy in the British Isles*, Vol.2, 1973

BRIGGS, R.W., *Chinese Wilson*, 1993

CALLAWAY, D.J., *Magnolias* 1994 (The most recent and authoritative work on the genus)

FORREST, G., *The Gardeners Chronicle* 1910

JOHNSTONE, G.H., *Asiatic Magnolias in Cultivation*, 1955

MILLAIS, J.G., *Magnolias*, 1927

Newsletter of the American Magnolia Society/Journal of the Magnolia Society, from 1964 onwards

Royal Botanic Gardens, Kew, World Checklist and Bibliography of Magnoliaceae, 1996

Royal Horticultural Society, Camellias and Magnolias, Conference Report, 1950

The Scottish Rock Garden Club, George Forrest, 1935

TRESEDER, N.D., *Magnolias*, 1978

Societies

THE MAGNOLIA SOCIETY

Membership is a must for anyone interested in magnolias. Founded in 1963, it now has approximately 600 members from 25 different countries. Along with other valuable benefits, *The Journal of The Magnolia Society, Magnolia,* is published twice a year. It contains articles written by leading authorities covering a wide range of related subjects.

You can find out more on the internet at http:// www. tallahassee.net/~magnolia

Or Contact:
THE MAGNOLIA SOCIETY
Roberta Davids Hagen (Secretary)6616 81st Street
Cabin John, Maryland USA 20818
Email Rhagen6902@aol.com.

THE ROYAL HORTICULTURAL SOCIETY
THE RHODODENDRON, CAMELLIA AND MAGNOLIA GROUP

The 12 branches spread throughout Britain have regular meetings and lectures on all three genera. A great opportunity to meet and converse with other enthusiasts. A superb yearbook is published which has articles of interest on Magnolias.

Contact:
Mrs. Josephine Warren
The Hon. Secretary
The Rhododendron, Camellia and Magnolia Group
Netherton
Buckland Monachorum
Yelverton
Devon PL20 7NL
England

Index

Acknowledgements

First and foremost I wish to express my gratitude to Maurice and Rosemary Foster whose infectious enthusiasm for plants is an inspiration to all that meet them.

To both Nigel Holman at Chyverton, and Philip Tregunna at Caerhays Castle in whose company I have spent many enjoyable hours looking at plants.

The Swiss trio of magnolia growers, Dr. Piet van Veen, Sir Peter Smithers and Otto and Gretel Eisenhut for sharing their great wealth of knowledge over many years.

My employer Mrs Dorte Semler Nielsen of Hascombe Court, who has allowed me to embellish her garden with my passion for plants.

I would like to give special thanks to The National Trust, The Royal Botanic Gardens, Kew, and the Crown Estate Commissioners (Windsor), not only for their permission to use pictures taken in their gardens, but for the years of pleasure I have had admiring their plant collections.

And finally to the staff at Hamlyn who have been a pleasure to work with.

Photographic Acknowledgements

The publishers would like to thank the Crown Estate Commissioners (Windsor) and Mrs Dorte Semler Nielsen of Hascombe Court for their permission to photograph their collections for the book.

Jacket. Octopus Publishing Group Ltd/Peter Myers
Bridgeman Art Library/By Courtesy of the Board of Trustees of the V & A 18 Top Left/Phillips, The International Fine Art Auctioneers 13/Victoria & Albert Museum, London, UK 10-11
B & B Photographs Professor Stefan Buczacki/69
Corbis UK Ltd/Lee Snider 6-7
Garden Picture Library/Howard Rice 34-35/JS Sira 43/Friedrich Strauss 64
Octopus Publishing Group Ltd./David Loftus title, 4-5, 14, 15, 24 Top, 30 Top, 30 Centre, 30 Bottom, 31 Top, 31 Bottom, 32 Top, 32 Centre 32 Bottom 33 Top, 33 Bottom, 37 Top, 37 Bottom, 38, 40-41, 47 Bottom, 48 Centre, 57 Top, 57 Bottom, 63, 66-67, 70 Bottom, 71, 80, 93 Bottom, 95 Bottom, 97, 103, 106, 108 Top Right, 109, 110, 121/Peter Myers half title, 22, 60-61, 62, 122-123/Frances Rankin 26, 27 Top, 27 Centre, 27 Bottom/Graham Rankin 9 Top Right, 12 Top, 12 Bottom Right, 19 Top, 24 Bottom, 25, 28, 29, 44, 46 Top, 50-51, 58, 59 Top, 59 Bottom, 68, 70 Top, 72 Top, 73, 76, 77 Top, 77 Bottom, 78, 79 Bottom, 82, 83 Bottom, 84 Bottom, 85 Top, 86 Bottom, 87, 88, 89 Top, 90 Bottom, 91 Top, 91 Bottom, 92 Top, 92 Bottom, 94, 95 Top, 96 Top/96 Bottom 99, 100 Top, 100 Bottom 101 Top 101 Bottom, 104 Top, 105, 108 Top Left, 108 Bottom, 111, 112 Top, 113, 114, 115, 116 Top 116 Bottom, 117 Top, 117 Bottom, 118, 119 Bottom
Maurice Foster 9 Top Left, 12 Bottom, 102
Natural Image/Bob Gibbons 20
Clive Nichols Photography 8
Graham Rankin 18 Bottom Right, 21, 36 (reproduced by kind permission of RHS Plant Centre, Wisley), 45, 54-55, 74-75, 79 Top, 81, 83 Top, 84 Top, 86 Top, 89 Bottom, 90 Top, 93 Top, 98 Bottom, 104 Bottom 107 112 Bottom 119 Top, 120
Royal Botanic Gardens, Kew 16-17
Tony Schilling/ 19 Bottom Right